JOE CELKO'S
Analytics and OLAP in SQL

Joe Celko

ELSEVIER

AMSTERDAM • BOSTON • HEIDELBERG • LONDON
NEW YORK • OXFORD • PARIS • SAN DIEGO
SAN FRANCISCO • SINGAPORE • SYDNEY • TOKYO
MORGAN KAUFMANN PUBLISHERS IS AN IMPRINT OF ELSEVIER

MORGAN KAUFMANN PUBLISHERS

Publisher	Diane Cerra
Publishing Services Manager	George Morrison
Editorial Assistant	Asma Palmeiro
Cover Design	Side by Side Studios
Cover Image	Side by Side Studios
Cover Designer	Eric DeCicco
Composition	Multiscience Press, Inc.
Copyeditor	Multiscience Press, Inc.
Proofreader	Multiscience Press, Inc.
Indexer	Multiscience Press, Inc.
Interior printer	The Maple-Vail Book Manufacturing Group
Cover printer	Phoenix Color Corp.

Morgan Kaufmann Publishers is an imprint of Elsevier.
500 Sansome Street, Suite 400, San Francisco, CA 94111

This book is printed on acid-free paper.

Library of Congress Cataloging-in-Publication Data

Application submitted.

ISBN-10 :   0123695120
ISBN-13:   978-0-12-369512-3

For information on all Morgan Kaufmann publications,
visit our Web site at www.mkp.com or www.books.elsevier.com

Printed in the United States of America
06 07 08 09 5 4 3 2 1

For Charlotte and Tess, who should have gotten a dedication
at least a decade ago for all the work they put into school.

CONTENTS

Introduction

Where is the wisdom?
Lost in the knowledge.
Where is the knowledge?
Lost is the information.
—T. S. Elliot (1888–1965)

Where is the information?
Lost in the data.
Where is the data?
Lost is the @#$%"& database!!
—Joe Celko (1947–)

Many years ago, I did a blank verse follow-up to a T. S. Eliot poem, which you see at the start of this introduction. What I want to do in this book is to move from data to information via analytics of various kinds. I am not so arrogant to assume that I can go from information to wisdom for the book after this—I leave wisdom and enlightenment to my wife, the Soto Zen monk.

Beyond Queries

The goal of this book is to go beyond my usual "How to write a query" book and get into online analytical processing (OLAP), or analytics, as well as data quality, data transformations, and the other tools outside the usual scope of a working programmer—I'd like to look at a bigger picture. I will not cover the topics in detail, but instead try to give you an overview of these techniques.

OLAP and data warehousing in SQL are a part of this, but they are not the only tools. I will try to stick to standard SQL and SQL/PSM in any code. However, much of this kind of work has to be done with third-party tools, such as report generators, statistical packages, data transformation tools, and so forth. I will break my usual pattern of using purely standard SQL and give overviews of commercial tools, but not in great detail. Any description of a particular release of a particular product would be dated in a few years at most, anyway.

Some of the Differences between OLAP and OLTP

Size

The first obvious difference between analytics and online transaction processing (OLTP) databases is the size of the data involved. Analytics wants to have as much data as possible from which to draw information. OLTP wants to be fast, which means running lean.

My first column in the information technology (IT) trade press was entitled "Program Tests Basic 'Rhino Algorithm'" (*Information Systems News*, September 8, 1980). The column talked about how Tarzan avoided being run over by rhinoceroses in the old movie. His algorithm was to jump to one side at the last minute so as to avoid becoming jungle road kill. It worked beautifully in every black and white Tarzan movie I ever saw as a kid. The problem with his algorithm was that it did not scale well to an entire herd of stampeding rhinoceroses.

Data Sources

The next difference is that analytics have multiple data sources. Data is spread out in many places within an enterprise, and these "local islands of data" are not going to be on the same platforms. It would not make sense to put a mainframe in every department or on every desktop; nor would it make sense to put a major corporate accounting system on a PC.

But you also want to use external data as well. For example, census data lets you plan inventory choices to match the people who will be shopping at each store branch.

Transactions versus Computations

The third major difference is that analytics do more computations than OLTP. Most of these computations are in the aggregate, rather than on single entities. You do not care that John Smith bought a candy bar from your store on Thursday. Your cash register system will capture that data and print out a receipt for Mr. Smith's transaction. In analytics, we want to find the purchase patterns for all candy bars in all our stores. The information we want from analytics often has a strong temporal component, rather than being a single event. We try to predict the future by using what we have learned about the past behavior of our system.

Volume and intended use make a big difference in the representation of data, the type of queries that are useful, and even how the information is physically stored.

Data Users

The OLTP system should be available to lots of users, even on the Internet. These users are customers, suppliers, and employees. They can be skilled workers, but they can also be an unspecified population. The interface is very important to them.

The OLAP system works with a small set of skilled users. They are more likely to be statisticians who know which algorithms to use. While nice displays are always appreciated, the OLAP user can handle specialized, often complicated, interfaces.

Queries

The OLTP system works with fast responses to relatively simple queries on particular entities. A typical query might be looking up your bank account balance and recent transactions.

The OLAP system can wait to receive detailed answers to complex queries. Speed is nice, but it is not as important as the depth of precision of the results. These queries are for groupings and categories of entities.

An online user submitting an order will not wait 30 seconds to see if the item is in stock, while an analyst will gladly wait 30 minutes to get a complete report of sales trends for all items for the last year.

Normalization

The OLTP system must be normalized so that as it changes, it preserves data integrity. Denormalizing for speed seldom is worth the loss in data integrity. You need declarative referential integrity (DRI) actions, triggers, assertions, and so forth to be sure that your data is valid. The schema should be at least third normal form (3NF), though we'd really like fifth normal form (5NF) and domain-key normal forms.

The OLAP system is static, so its data must have integrity before it goes into the schema. It is not going to change while it is in use. The OLAP system works with a star schema or snowflake schema, which are highly denormalized but have data integrity because they are static.

Also, normalization prevents redundancy, and redundancy destroys data integrity in OLTP. Redundancy can speed up queries in OLAP.

Query Tools and Computers

The OLTP system favors a highly portable SQL. It needs to be deployed quickly and available to a wide range of users if it is successful.

The OLAP system favors SQL, but it needs statistical extensions and will also use statistical packages (SAS, SPSS, and specialized products. Once a data warehouse is in place, it does not change.

While the SQL-99 standard OLAP features are being supported in DB2, Oracle, Mimer, and other SQL products, there comes a point where you need other tools.

SQL can run on a general computer, but you will find the OLAP system does much better with a very large database (VLDB) product whose architecture is built to handle massive amounts of data with totally different access methods.

The poor SQL programmer who has grown up in the OLTP world is suddenly as helpless in the OLAP world as the procedural programmer who was dropped into a nonprocedural SQL world. It does not feel good to begin the work day with "Everything I know is wrong" written on your t-shirt.

Corrections and Additions

Please send any corrections, additions, suggestions, improvements, or alternative solutions to me or to the publisher.

Morgan-Kaufmann Publishers
500 Sansome Street #400
San Francisco, CA 94111-3211

CHAPTER 1

Basic Reports and History

Prisoner: Where am I?
Number Two: In the Village.
Prisoner: What do you want?
Number Two: Information.
Prisoner: Which side are you on?
Number Two: That would be telling. We want information,
    information, information . . .
Prisoner: You won't get it.
Number Two: By hook or by crook we will.
Prisoner: Who are you?
Number Two: The new Number Two.
Prisoner: Who is Number One?
Number Two: You are Number Six.
Prisoner: I am not a number. I am a free man.
Number Two: Ha, ha, ha, ha . . .
—*The Prisoner* (1967)

O NCE UPON A time, long, long ago, we had punch cards and magnetic tapes for data processing. We printed reports onto paper. There were no databases or cheap video terminals. Instead we produced tons of continuous-form paper outputs, and I do mean tons.

The problem was that nobody read these reports. In fact, there was a standard trick in software engineering consulting in the 1980s to find out about the usage. You took one of these huge stacks of paper and inserted an envelope with a $10 bill in the middle of the report. The note told the person who opened the envelope to keep the money and return the note, which had the name of the report on it, to the consultant. Only about one out of 10 or 12 envelopes were discovered.

Data was failing to be turned into information. People simply got a sense of security and importance from looking at a large stack of paper. When hardcopy reports were used, it was usually just the summary-level data. The whole report would sit around in a binder until the next time it was run. The new report would replace the old in the binder, and a few summary pages would be put into a second binder.

If the report did not give you the data in a format you could use, you had to reformat it by hand with a calculator. Later on, you would use a spreadsheet, but the idea was the same.

The reason for all of this was that computers and computer time were very costly, and display terminals were years away. Running a paper report once and letting people share it was the economical sound decision.

1.1 Cases

The simplest possible report is a printout of each record on a separate page or in a few lines on a case-by-case basis. In the old days, however, you could not afford to run a program to print a few pages on demand. We would print out a set of these cases with a date on them, do updates manually, and then key in the changes in batches. The real "database" was a vertical filing cabinet.

This meant that you had to have a sorting key that defined the order of the output. This usually meant alphabetical or numerical order on one or more fields. The classic example is a printed telephone book. If you know a name and alphabetical order, it is quite easy. However, if you wanted to find all the people who live on Elm Street, you would want to get the same data in a very different order.

People do not appreciate the power of alphabetical ordering for data. Hong Kong telephone operators commit thousands of names and numbers to memory because Chinese does not have a way to map sounds to characters.

Much of the computer time in the early days of data processing was spent sorting data to get reports in the desired order. Since magnetic tapes are sequential by their physical nature, we got very good at merging and sorting algorithms. This also meant that we assumed that all data had to be in sequential order and that we needed to have a physical sort key.

This assumption became the *primary key* in SQL. By the time we realized that a relational key has nothing to do with the physical ordering of the data's storage, and that all keys are equally keys, the language was defined.

Today, cases can be called up on a screen and updated instantly. But, even more significantly, you do not have to use one sort key to get to the data.

1.2   Control-Break Reports

The next type of report goes by several names: control-break or banded reports are the most common. They consist of lines of detailed information, followed by summary information at various levels of aggregation. The assumption is that your data falls into a hierarchy. Today, a dimension hierarchy is just another type of control break. Like the alphabet, hierarchies are a useful way to organize data. Some things don't change, they simply get mechanized.

Its layout was determined by the hardware that we originally used to produce these reports. The electronic accounting machines had a limited number of accumulators and almost no internal data storage. A record was read from a deck of cards (later from a magnetic tape) and printed on the output paper, and the relevant fields were added to the accumulators as the data passed through the hardware. When the record that started the next group was read, the accumulator contents was output and reset. The number of levels of aggregation was determined by the hardware.

The way that people actually used these reports was to ignore the details and flip the stack of paper to the final summary pages. The grand totals were on the last pages, so people would put them into a binder and throw everything else out.

The obvious way to design such a report would have been to start with the grand totals, then move to subtotals, then sub-subtotals, and finally to the details. Today, this is what is done with terminals and drill-down displays.

1.3   Cross-Tabulation Reports

The third most common report is a cross-tabulation report, also known as "crosstabs" in statistics. This has become more important, because it is the basis for cubes and other OLAP storage methods, which we will discuss later.

A simple crosstabs is an array of cells on at least two attributes. The values of one attribute go on the horizontal axis, and the values of the other attribute go on the vertical axis. Each cell has a statistic about the cases for the entities that have both values. For example, a sex by race crosstabs would have a total count for white females, white males, black females, black males, and so forth.

Most such reports also include row and column totals, such as males and females, and a total for each racial category. While simple counts are the most common statistic used, you can also compute averages, extrema, and more powerful statistics such as chi-squares.

Interactive packages, such as Brio, allow the user to arrange and trim the grid with interactive tools.

1.4 Presentation Graphics

The fourth kind of report was not very popular in the old days, because it had to be drawn by hand. These were the graphic presentations, such as pie charts, bar charts, and line charts.

The early computers did not have the output devices to do these things for us. I am not going to bother with a discussion of this type of report for two reasons. The first reason is that I am more concerned with data that is represented in a purely computerized format and ways to manipulate it within a computer.

The second reason is that the best material about this type of report has been presented by Edward Tufte in his books and courses (http://www.edwardtufte.com). His book, *The Visual Display of Quantitative Information*, is a classic that anyone who works with data should own. Stephen Few (www.perceptualedge.com) is also writing good stuff on information presentation.

1.5 Local Databases

The final kind of report is not really a traditional report at all. Personal computers and mass storage are cheap. We can send the user a small, almost personal database of his or her own to use on a local machine as he or she sees fit. This is not the same thing as sending a report to the user that cannot be altered. We download raw data from a trusted source, usually a central company database.

The user can be a subscriber who gets new data on a regular basis from a central data source. This is handy for things that have a regular schedule, such as monthly inventory changes or sales leads. One of the best examples of this kind of reporting is continuous stock market downloads. The raw data comes from a service and gets formatted and analyzed locally by the subscriber's program.

The other model is to download data on request, but the idea of local report generation is still the same. The most common example of this is the Internet. You probably do not think of it as a reporting service.

In recent years, companies have also set up servers that do nothing but provide reports.

CHAPTER
2
Cross-Tabulations

A CROSS-TABULATION, or crosstabs for short, is a common statistical report. It can be done in IBM's QMF tool, using the ACROSS summary option, and in many other SQL-based reporting packages. SPSS, SAS, and other statistical packages have library procedures or language constructs for crosstabs. Many spreadsheets can load the results of SQL queries and perform a crosstabs within the spreadsheet. You can even do it with Microsoft Access (the poor man's analytics) crosstab queries!

If you can use a reporting package on the server in a client/server system instead of the following method, do so. It will run faster and in less space than the method discussed here. However, if you have to use the reporting package on the client side, the extra time required to transfer data will make these methods on the server side much faster.

A crosstabs takes the values in a column, turns them into columns in the report. For example, if you have a table with Sales data, a crosstabs would have columns for each year that appears in the sales date "year" axis and the product codes as rows on the other "Products" axis. The following SQL code is based on a trick that mathematician call an identity matrix. When you do a CROSS JOIN with the CrossTabs table, you multiply a value by one if you want to keep it and multiply by 0 if you want to drop the value.

```
CREATE TABLE Sales
(product_name CHAR(15) NOT NULL,
 product_price DECIMAL(5,2) NOT NULL,
 qty INTEGER NOT NULL,
 sales_year INTEGER NOT NULL);

CREATE TABLE Crosstabs
(year INTEGER NOT NULL,
 year1 INTEGER NOT NULL,
 year2 INTEGER NOT NULL,
 year3 INTEGER NOT NULL,
 year4 INTEGER NOT NULL,
 year5 INTEGER NOT NULL,
 row_total INTEGER NOT NULL);
```

The table would be populated as follows:

Sales_year	year1	year2	year3	year4	year5	row_total
1990	1	0	0	0	0	1
1991	0	1	0	0	0	1
1992	0	0	1	0	0	1
1993	0	0	0	1	0	1
1994	0	0	0	0	1	1

The query to produce the report table is:

```
SELECT S1.product_name,
    SUM(S1.qty * S1.product_price * C1.year1),
    SUM(S1.qty * S1.product_price * C1.year2),
    SUM(S1.qty * S1.product_price * C1.year3),
    SUM(S1.qty * S1.product_price * C1.year4),
    SUM(S1.qty * S1.product_price * C1.year5),
    SUM(S1.qty * S1.product_price * C1.row_total)
FROM Sales AS S1, Crosstabs AS C1
WHERE S1.year = C1.year
GROUP BY S1.product_name;
```

Obviously, (S1.product_price * S1.qty) is the total dollar amount of each product in each year. The yearN column will be either a 1 or a 0. If it is a 0, the total dollar amount in the SUM() is 0; if it is a 1, the total dollar amount in the SUM() is unchanged.

This solution lets you adjust the time frame being shown in the report by replacing the values in the year column to whichever consecutive years you wish. A two-way crosstabs takes two variables and produces a spreadsheet with all values of one variable in the rows and all values of the other represented by the columns. Each cell in the table holds the COUNT of entities that have those values for the two variables. NULLs will not fit into a crosstabs very well, unless you decide to make them a group of their own.

Another trick is to use the POSITION() function to convert a string into a 1 or a 0. For example, assume we have a "day of the week" function that returns a three-letter abbreviation, and we want to report the sales of items by day of the week in a horizontal list.

```
CREATE TABLE Weekdays
(day_name CHAR(3) NOT NULL PRIMARY KEY,
 mon INTEGER NOT NULL,
 tue INTEGER NOT NULL,
 wed INTEGER NOT NULL,
 thu INTEGER NOT NULL,
 fri INTEGER NOT NULL,
 sat INTEGER NOT NULL,
 sun INTEGER NOT NULL);

INSERT INTO WeekDays
VALUES ('MON', 1, 0, 0, 0, 0, 0, 0),
       ('TUE', 0, 1, 0, 0, 0, 0, 0),
       ('WED', 0, 0, 1, 0, 0, 0, 0),
       ('THU', 0, 0, 0, 1, 0, 0, 0),
       ('FRI', 0, 0, 0, 0, 1, 0, 0),
       ('SAT', 0, 0, 0, 0, 0, 1, 0),
       ('SUN', 0, 0, 0, 0, 0, 0, 1);

SELECT item,
       SUM(amt * qty * mon
           * POSITION('MON' IN DOW(sales_date))) AS mon_tot,
       SUM(amt * qty * tue
           * POSITION('TUE' IN DOW(sales_date))) AS tue_tot,
       SUM(amt * qty * wed
           * POSITION('WED' IN DOW(sales_date))) AS wed_tot,
```

```
    SUM(amt * qty* thu
        * POSITION('THU' IN DOW(sales_date))) AS thu_tot,
    SUM(amt * qty * fri
        * POSITION('FRI' IN DOW(sales_date))) AS fri_tot,
    SUM(amt * qty * sat
        * POSITION('SAT' IN DOW(sales_date))) AS sat_tot,
    SUM(amt * qty * sun
        * POSITION('SUN' IN DOW(sales_date))) AS sun_tot
  FROM Weekdays, Sales;
```

There are also totals for each column and each row, as well as a grand total. Crosstabs of (n) variables are defined by building an n-dimensional spreadsheet. But you cannot easily print (n) dimensions on two-dimensional paper. The usual trick is to display the results as a two-dimensional grid with one or both axes as a tree structure. The way the values are nested on the axis is usually under program control; thus, "race within sex" shows sex broken down by race, whereas "sex within race" shows race broken down by sex.

Assume that we have a table, Personnel (emp_nbr, sex, race, job_nbr, salary_amt), keyed on employee number, with no NULLs in any columns. We wish to write a crosstabs of employees by sex and race, which would look like this:

	asian	black	caucasian	hispanic	Other	TOTALS
Male	3	2	12	5	5	27
Female	1	10	20	2	9	42
TOTAL	4	12	32	7	14	69

The first thought is to use a GROUP BY and write a simple query, thus:

```
SELECT sex, race, COUNT(*)
  FROM Personnel
 GROUP BY sex, race;
```

This approach works fine for two variables and would produce a table that could be sent to a report writer program to give a final version. But where are your column and row totals? This means you also need to write these two queries:

```
SELECT race, COUNT(*) FROM Personnel GROUP BY race;
SELECT sex, COUNT(*) FROM Personnel GROUP BY sex;
```

However, what I wanted was a table with a row for males and a row for females, with columns for each of the racial groups, just as I drew it.

But let us assume that we want to break this information down within a third variable, say job code. I want to see the job_nbr and the total by sex and race within each job code. Our query set starts to get bigger and bigger. A crosstabs can also include other summary data, such as total or average salary within each cell of the table.

2.1   Crosstabs by Cross-Join

A solution proposed by John M. Baird of Datapoint, in San Antonio, Texas, involves creating a matrix table for each variable in the crosstabs, thus:

```
SexMatrix
sex   Male Female
========_=========
'M'    1   0
'F'    0   1


RaceMatrix
race        asian  black  caucasian  hispanic  Other
=====================================================

asian         1      0        0          0        0
black         0      1        0          0        0
caucasian     0      0        1          0        0
hispanic      0      0        0          1        0
Other         0      0        0          0        1
```

The query then constructs the cells by using a CROSS JOIN (Cartesian product) and summation for each one, thus:

```
SELECT job_nbr,
    SUM(asian * male) AS AsianMale,
    SUM(asian * female) AS AsianFemale,
    SUM(black * male) AS BlackMale,
    SUM(black * female) AS BlackFemale,
    SUM(cauc * male) AS CaucMale,
```

```
        SUM(cauc * female) AS CaucFemale,
        SUM(hisp * male) AS HispMale,
        SUM(hisp * female) AS HispFemale,
        SUM(other * male) AS OtherMale,
        SUM(other * female) AS OtherFemale
   FROM Personnel, SexMatrix, RaceMatrix
  WHERE (RaceMatrix.race = Personnel.race)
    AND (SexMatrix.sex = Personnel.sex)
  GROUP BY job_nbr;
```

Numeric summary data can be obtained from this table. For example, the total salary for each cell can be computed by SUM(<race> * <sex> * salary) AS <cell name> in place of what we have here.

2.2   Crosstabs by Outer Joins

Another method, invented by Jim Panttaja, uses a series of temporary tables or VIEWs and then combines them with OUTER JOINs.

```
CREATE VIEW Guys (race, male_tally)
AS SELECT race, COUNT(*)
     FROM Personnel
     WHERE sex = 'M'
     GROUP BY race;
```

Correspondingly, you could have written:

```
CREATE VIEW Dolls (race, female_tally)
AS SELECT race, COUNT(*)
     FROM Personnel
     WHERE sex = 'F'
     GROUP BY race;
```

But they can be combined for a crosstabs, without column and row totals, like this:

```
SELECT Guys.race, male_tally, female_tally
  FROM Guys LEFT OUTER JOIN Dolls
       ON Guys.race = Dolls.race;
```

The idea is to build a starting column in the crosstabs, then progressively add columns to it. You use the LEFT OUTER JOIN to avoid missing-data problems.

2.3   Crosstabs by Subquery

Another method takes advantage of the orthogonality of correlated subqueries in SQL-92. Think about what each row or column in the crosstabs wants.

```
SELECT DISTINCT race,
      (SELECT COUNT(*)
         FROM Personnel AS P1
        WHERE P0.race = P1.race
          AND sex = 'M') AS male_tally,
      (SELECT COUNT(*)
         FROM Personnel AS P2
        WHERE P0.race = P2.race
          AND sex = 'F') AS female_tally
  FROM Personnel AS P0;
```

An advantage of this approach is that you can attach another column to get the row tally by adding:

```
(SELECT COUNT(*)
   FROM Personnel AS P3
  WHERE P0.race = P3.race) AS race_tally
```

Likewise, to get the column tallies, union the previous query with:

```
SELECT  'Summary',
      (SELECT COUNT(*)
         FROM Personnel
        WHERE sex = 'M') AS male_grandtotal,
      (SELECT COUNT(*)
         FROM Personnel
        WHERE sex = 'F') AS female_grandtotal,
      (SELECT COUNT(*)
         FROM Personnel) AS grandtotal
  FROM Personnel;
```

2.4   Crosstabs by CASE Expression

Probably the best method is to use the CASE expression. If you need to get the final row of the traditional crosstabs, you can add:

```
SELECT sex,
    SUM(CASE race WHEN 'caucasian' THEN 1 ELSE 0 END) AS
caucasian,
    SUM(CASE race WHEN 'black' THEN 1 ELSE 0 END) AS black,
    SUM(CASE race WHEN 'asian' THEN 1 ELSE 0 END) AS asian,
    SUM(CASE race WHEN 'latino' THEN 1 ELSE 0 END) AS latino,
    SUM(CASE race WHEN 'other' THEN 1 ELSE 0 END) AS other,
    COUNT(*) AS row_total
FROM Personnel
GROUP BY sex
UNION ALL
SELECT '      ',
    SUM(CASE race WHEN 'caucasian' THEN 1 ELSE 0 END),
    SUM(CASE race WHEN 'black' THEN 1 ELSE 0 END),
    SUM(CASE race WHEN 'asian' THEN 1 ELSE 0 END),
    SUM(CASE race WHEN 'latino' THEN 1 ELSE 0 END),
    SUM(CASE race WHEN 'other' THEN 1 ELSE 0 END),
    COUNT(*) AS column_total
FROM Personnel;
```

2.5   Crosstabs with Row and Column Summaries

Given an array, you can do row and column statistics using the following view:

```
CREATE TABLE Array
(i INTEGER NOT NULL
   CHECK (i BETWEEN 1 AND 3),
 j INTEGER NOT NULL
  CHECK (j BETWEEN 1 AND 3),
cell_value INTEGER DEFAULT 0 NOT NULL,
PRIMARY KEY(i, j)); -- this is the natural key

INSERT INTO Array(i,j,cell_value)
VALUES (1, 1, 5), (1, 2, 2), (1, 3, 7),
       (2, 1, 2), (2, 2, 7), (2, 3, 5),
       (3, 1, 9), (3, 2, 10), (3, 3, 8);
```

```
CREATE VIEW CrossTabs (i, j, ij_tot, i_tot, j_tot)
AS
SELECT i, j, cell_value,
      (SELECT SUM(cell_value) FROM Array),
      (SELECT SUM(A1.cell_value)
         FROM Array AS A1
        WHERE A1.i = Array.i),
      (SELECT SUM(A1.cell_value)
         FROM Array AS A1
        WHERE A1.j = Array.j)
FROM Array;
```

```
CrossTabs
i  j cell_value ij_tot i_tot j_tot
==================================
1  1       5         55     14     16
1  2       2         55     14     19
1  3       7         55     14     20
2  1       2         55     14     16
2  2       7         55     14     19
2  3       5         55     14     20
3  1       9         55     27     16
3  2      10         55     27     19
3  3       8         55     27     20
```

Having the grand total (ij_tot) in a column is actually an advantage, because you often compute the percentages of the cells to the corresponding grand total, row total, and column total. It is also reasonable to assume that a modern optimizer will be able to compute the subquery expressions in a single pass.

CHAPTER 3

Dimension Tables

DIMENSIONS CAN BE tricky. We would like as much granularity as possible, but not so fine as to make summarizing the fact table data a task that produces little information. For the sake of discussion, let's assume we have a vaguely defined retail store's data warehouse. At one extreme, we could have a single "Product" value. At that point, since every row in the fact table has only that value, why bother to store it at all?

At the other extreme, we could break products down by manufacturer, then by item within manufacturer, since this is contained in the UPC code. But we could also add the manufacturer's package numbers, which relate to production dates, expiration dates, and production batches. However, this is a lot of information to track.

The vehicle identification number (VIN) for automobiles actually contains data at that level, and for an automobile it is worth tracking. But it is a bit much for a candy bar sale in a data warehouse. The appropriate choice of granularity requires adequate understanding of the business problems and the questions that will be asked.

3.1 Star and Snowflake Schemas

The star schema or dimensional model invented by Ralph Kimball and his work with data warehouses. The idea is that you have a large fact table with much smaller dimensional tables joined to it. Now we need to define these terms.

Each row in a fact table models a complete fact about some event that occurred in the enterprise. It is not about entities and relationships, like the rows in a table in an OLTP database. The fact table is denormalized and usually has a temporal element, since events have to exist in time.

The purpose of normalization in an OLTP schema is data integrity. That means that when the data changes because of an INSERT, UPDATE, or DELETE statement, the schema maintains the proper relationships. The best way to think of normalization in a star schema is to forget most of them and start thinking in a dimensional model.

The fact tables in a star schema tend to have lots of rows. (See Figure 3.1.) One or more of the columns will be a temporal dimension of some kind, such as the date of a sale. The other dimensions can be values drawn from some domain. We will discuss kinds of scales later. There is a REFERENCE from the fact table to each appropriate dimension table.

A degenerate dimension or surrogate fact key is one that exists in the fact table, but has no reference to a dimension table. These are used to identify a row and are usually generated inside the schema as a shorter way to reference a particular row without having to use the compound key in the fact table.

Let's make this more concrete. In an OLTP database, you might have separate tables for customers, products, the orders that were placed, and so forth. In a fact table, you would have a row that might tell you that "Customer A bought product B on date C at store D using payment method E with a loyalty card F"—an entire fact in one row.

The other interesting thing about a fact table is that you do not process transactions against it. These facts are history, and, unlike the leaders of the former Soviet Union, we do not rewrite it on the fly. The assumption is that you screen the data when you load it to be sure that it is at least consistent and, even better, correct. The data stays unchanged in the fact table until it gets to be old enough to be archived or discarded.

This is why you don't need normalization or constraints to protect the data integrity. The data is scrubbed, checked, validated, and fixed once it is in the star schema. Instead, the problem is how to summarize and aggregate the facts to get information out of the star schema.

The fact tables are huge compared with the dimensions. They are usually huge compared with anything you have had in an OLTP database. This makes sense, because they model a history of completed events rather than a snapshot of current transactions. One of the largest

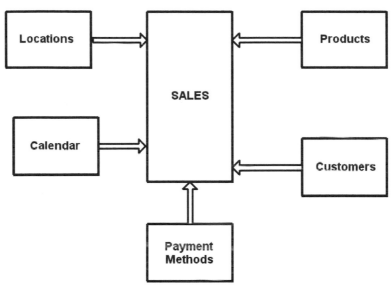

Figure 3.1 Simple Star Schema for Sales Fact Table

data warehouses on earth is used by Wal-Mart. It is measured in petabytes (thousands of terabytes) and holds more than one and a half years of facts at the level of individual sales.

Snowflake schemas have a dimension that is broken down into "special cases." (See Figure 3.2) The main dimension holds the common information, and the arms of the snowflake hold details that apply only to particular subspecies. Object-oriented programmers will think of the classic scenario that calls for a root class with common attributes with specialized subclasses under it.

As an example, let's take a class of vehicles, find an industry-standard identifier (VIN), and then add two mutually exclusive subclasses, sport utility vehicles ('SUV') and all-terrain vehicles ('ATV').

```
CREATE TABLE Vehicles
(vin CHAR(17) NOT NULL PRIMARY KEY,
 vehicle_type CHAR(3) NOT NULL
      CHECK(vehicle_type IN ('SUV', 'ATV')),
  fuel_type  CHAR(4) NOT NULL
   CHECK (door_count >= 0),
 UNIQUE (vin, vehicle_type),
 ..);
```

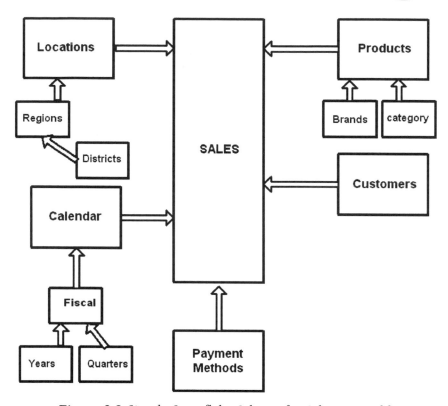

Figure 3.2 Simple Snowflake Schema for Sales Fact Table

Notice the overlapping candidate keys. I then use a compound candidate key (vin, vehicle_type) and a constraint in each subclass table to assure that the vehicle_type is locked and agrees with the vehicles table. Add some DRI actions and you are done:

```
CREATE TABLE SUVs
(vin CHAR(17) NOT NULL PRIMARY KEY,
 vehicle_type CHAR(3) DEFAULT 'SUV' NOT NULL
      CHECK(vehicle_type = 'SUV'),
 UNIQUE (vin, vehicle_type),
 FOREIGN KEY (vin, vehicle_type)
  REFERENCES Vehicles(vin, vehicle_type)
  ON UPDATE CASCADE
  ON DELETE CASCADE,
 ..);

CREATE TABLE ATMs
(vin CHAR(17) NOT NULL PRIMARY KEY,
```

```
vehicle_type CHAR(3) DEFAULT 'ATV' NOT NULL
      CHECK(vehicle_type = 'ATV'),
UNIQUE (vin, vehicle_type),
FOREIGN KEY (vin, vehicle_type)
 REFERENCES Vehicles(vin, vehicle_type)
 ON UPDATE CASCADE
 ON DELETE CASCADE,
..);
```

I can continue to build a hierarchy like this. For example, if I had an ATMs table that broke down into sub-types of ATM class vehicles, my schema might look like this:

```
CREATE TABLE ATMs
(vin CHAR(17) NOT NULL PRIMARY KEY,
 vehicle_type CHAR(3) DEFAULT 'ATV' NOT NULL
      CHECK(vehicle_type IN ('3WH', '4WH', 'ATV')),
 UNIQUE (vin, vehicle_type),
 FOREIGN KEY (vin, vehicle_type)
  REFERENCES Vehicles(vin, vehicle_type)
  ON UPDATE CASCADE
  ON DELETE CASCADE,
 ..);

CREATE TABLE ThreeWheels
(vin CHAR(17) NOT NULL PRIMARY KEY,
 vehicle_type CHAR(3) DEFAULT '3WH' NOT NULL
      CHECK(vehicle_type = '3WH'),
 UNIQUE (vin, vehicle_type),
 FOREIGN KEY (vin, vehicle_type)
  REFERENCES ATMans(vin, vehicle_type)
  ON UPDATE CASCADE
  ON DELETE CASCADE,
 ..);

CREATE TABLE FourWheel
(vin CHAR(17) NOT NULL PRIMARY KEY,
 vehicle_type CHAR(3) DEFAULT '4WH' NOT NULL
      CHECK(vehicle_type = '4WH'),
 UNIQUE (vin, vehicle_type),
 FOREIGN KEY (vin, vehicle_type)
```

```
REFERENCES ATMans (vin, vehicle_type)
ON UPDATE CASCADE
ON DELETE CASCADE,
..);
```

The idea is to build a chain of identifiers and types in a UNIQUE() constraint that go up the tree when you use a REFERENCES constraint. Obviously, you can do variants of this trick to get different class structures.

If an entity doesn't have to be exclusively one subtype, you play with the root of the class hierarchy:

```
CREATE TABLE Vehicles
(vin CHAR(17) NOT NULL,
 vehicle_type CHAR(3) NOT NULL
      CHECK(vehicle_type IN ('SUV', 'ATV')),
 PRIMARY KEY (vin, vehicle_type),
 ..);
```

Now, start hiding all this stuff in VIEWs immediately and add an INSTEAD OF trigger to those VIEWs.

3.2 Kinds of Dimensions

So how do we do summary and aggregation? The way we do everything in an Relational Data Base Management System (RDBMS) model of the world; we join tables to each other. Each of the attributes that we can summarize or aggregate is called a dimension. Much like scales and measurements in the OLTP world, dimensions come in many flavors.

The first issue is the granularity of the dimension. How fine a measurement do you put into the fact table? The time dimension is so basic and so well standardized that virtually every data warehouse has one. But one data model might want to keep sales by the day, and another might want to go to the hourly granularity. On the other end of the scale, the coarsest unit might be a year for one project and a multiyear period for another.

It is better to err on the side of finer granularity at the start. Dimension tables are small, and a few extra units are easy to store and have virtually no impact on performance. The real issue is the size of the fact table and how much it costs to store the extra granularity.

3.2.1 Slowly Changing Dimensions

Over time, the values of the attributes of a dimension table may change. For example, every few years, the Dewey decimal classification (DDC) system for libraries gets updated a bit and stays that way for a while. This is what Ralph Kimball calls *slowly changing dimensions* (SCDs). There are three ways to handle these situations.

1. *Type one SCD*: Overwrite the old values with the new ones. This is not a good answer to the problem unless we have found that the original data was wrong or that the new encoding is backward compatible.

2. *Type two SCD*: Add a new row containing the new value(s) and use a pair of (start_date, end_date) columns that tell you when each scale was in effect. An example of this would be a genuine change in a status—death, marriage, graduation, and so forth. This is usually the practical one to implement.

3. *Type three SCD*: Add a new attribute to the existing rows. One example of this is the change in 2005 in the United States from the old 10-digit Universal Product Code (UPC) to the 13-digit European Article Number (EAN) code on retail product barcodes. These codes are maintained by GS1 US (see the Uniform Code Council), and the details are available from their Web site. The reason for going back in time in this case is to make reporting easier.

3.2.2 Hierarchical Dimensions

This is self-explanatory; there is a hierarchy of units in the dimension. The most common examples are temporal, spatial, and geographical dimensions. In the geographical dimensions, ZIP codes aggregate into counties, counties into states, and states into nations. In temporal dimensions, hours aggregate into days, days into weeks, weeks into months, months into years, and so forth.

But notice that a dimension can have multiple hierarchies on it. Several years ago I consulted for a shoe company. The reporting hierarchy for the manufacturing side of the house had a very constant hierarchy based on physical materials and assembly. The marketing people were changing categories constantly based on fads and market research. On the manufacturing side, steel-toe work boots were one product. On the marketing side, they were two products based on size; the two distinct groups wearing them were construction workers with big feet and Goth girls with small feet. They did not shop at the same stores. And the market for average-size steel-toe work boots was about nil. The same example is used in Chapter 14.

I recommended using the nested sets model for hierarchies. This is discussed in detail in my other book, Joe Celko's *Trees and Hierarchies in SQL for Smarties* (2004, ISBN 1-55860-920-2) but let me give you a quick tutorial on this approach. Let me use geographical regions which have a natural physical hierarchy.

```
CREATE TABLE Regions_Dim
(region_name CHAR(10) NOT NULL PRIMARY KEY,
  lft INTEGER NOT NULL UNIQUE CHECK (lft > 0),
  rgt INTEGER NOT NULL UNIQUE CHECK (rgt > 1),
  CONSTRAINT order_okay CHECK (lft < rgt),
  Etc.);
```

```
Region_Dim
```

region_name	lft	rgt
'Nation'	1	12
'Georgia	2	3
'Texas'	4	11
'Dallas'	5	6
'Houston'	7	8
'Austin'	9	10

To show a tree as nested sets, replace the nodes with ovals, and then nest subordinate ovals inside each other. The root will be the largest oval and will contain every other node. The leaf nodes will be the innermost ovals with nothing else inside them, and the nesting will show the hierarchical relationship. The (lft, rgt) columns (I cannot use the reserved words LEFT and RIGHT in SQL) are what show the nesting. This is like XML, HTML, or parentheses.

This has some predictable results that we can use for building queries. The root is always (left = 1, right = 2 * (SELECT COUNT(*) FROM TreeTable)); leaf nodes always have (left + 1 = right); and subtrees are defined by the BETWEEN predicate. Here are four common queries that can be used to build others:

1.   A region and all of its containing regions, no matter how deep the tree.

```
SELECT R2.region_name, S1.*
   FROM Regions_Dim AS R1, Regions_Dim AS R2,
        Sales AS S1
  WHERE R1.lft BETWEEN R2.lft AND R2.rgt
    AND R1.region_name = S1.region_name;
```

2.   The region and all of its subdivisions. There is a nice symmetry here.

```
SELECT R1.region_name, S1.*
  FROM Regions_Dim AS R1, Regions_Dim AS R2,
       Sales AS S1
 WHERE R1.lft BETWEEN R2.lft AND R2.rgt
   AND R2.region_name = S1.region_name;
```

3.   Add a GROUP BY and aggregate functions to these basic queries, and you have hierarchical reports. For example, the totals at each level of the regional hierarch is given by this query:

```
SELECT R2.region_name, SUM(S1.sales_amt)
   FROM Regions_Dim AS R1, Regions_Dim AS R2,
        Sales AS S1
  WHERE R1.lft BETWEEN R2.lft AND R2.rgt
    AND R1.region_name = S1.region_name
  GROUP BY R2.region_name;
```

4.   Find the level of each region, so you can print the tree as an indented listing. Technically, you should declare a cursor to go with the ORDER BY clause.

```
SELECT COUNT(R2.region_name) AS level_nbr,
R1.region_name
   FROM Regions_Dim AS R1, Regions_Dim AS R2
  WHERE R1.lft BETWEEN R2.lft AND R2.rgt
  GROUP BY R1.lft, R1.region_name
  ORDER BY R1.lft;
```

The nested set model has an implied ordering of siblings that can also have meaning in reports. You probably want to put a level number directly in the dimension table, along with other structural information. Some obvious extra attributes in this example are the political unit (federal, state, county, city) and demographic classifications.

Please notice that you do not usually store a computed column in a table in an OLTP database. But in a data warehouse, you may want to do joins instead of computations, because they are faster for millions of rows. SQL engines designed for VLDB applications and data warehousing use special indexes, bit vectors, hashing, pointer chains, and other tricks to "pre-join" tables.

As an example of special optimizations, DB2 has an optimizer routine to detect a star schema. It builds a CROSS JOIN on the dimension tables to create a working table with a compound key. It then does a JOIN on the compound key. This assumes that the dimension table's cross-join is "small" in comparison to the available main storage.

3.2.3   Categorical Dimensions

This is also self-explanatory. The codes are discrete categories that usually expand over time to cover more and more cases. Very often a "miscellaneous" category starts to get larger and becomes worth splitting into more exact categories. But the "miscellaneous," "unknown," "N/A," and other missing data categories are often worth retaining.

Categories can be ordered ("high," "medium," "low") or unordered ("red," "green," "blue"). To complicate things more, there can be rules for transition from one state to another. For example, a barrel of grape juice can become wine or vinegar over time, but wine does not go back to grape juice.

The difficult part of this type of dimension is that setting up categories is not obvious in the real world, and the categories can change over time. When was the last time you saw music sales that included "Disco" as a category?

3.3   Calendars and Temporal Data

Sometimes the requirements for the time dimension are very fine-grained. Clifford Simak wrote a science fiction novel entitled *Time Is the Simplest Thing* by Clifford D. Simak (July 1977, ISBN: 0-84390480-1 Dorchester Publishing Company). He was wrong. The problems did not start with the Y2K problems we had in 2000, either. The calendar is irregular, and the only standard unit of time is the second; years, months, weeks, hours, minutes, and so forth are not part of the metric system but are mentioned in the ISO standards as conventions.

When working with times in an OLAP environment, keep all times in Universal Coordinated Time (UTC) and display them in ISO-8601 format (i.e., "yyyy-mm-dd hh:mm:ss.sss"). Now set up a dimension table to convert UTC to the local lawful time. That means you need to know the time zone of the data and whether or not they use Daylight Saving Time (DST) on a particular date.

```
CREATE TABLE TimeZoneDIM
(timezone_name CHAR(5) NOT NULL PRIMARY KEY
    CHECK (timezone_name SIMILAR TO '[A-Z][A-Z][A-Z]-[DS]
 utc_displacement DECIMAL(5,3) NOT NULL,
 dst_start_date DATE NOT NULL,
 dst_end_date DATE NOT NULL);
```

The suffix on the three-letter time zone name is D for Daylight Saving Time and S for Standard Time. There are still some places in the world with "fraction of an hour" displacements, so we need to use DECIMAL(s,p) data type.

While temporal dimensions can be made into hierarchies (years are made of quarters, quarters are made of months, months are made of weeks, weeks are made of days, and so forth), the calendar has cycles that other hierarchies do not. These reoccurring events do not fall neatly into simple patterns, because the cycles are not in synchronization. For example, in 2006, St. Patrick's Day (March 17, a fixed-date holiday) and Lent (a solar-lunar holiday, varying among Orthodox Christian churches) fell on the same Friday. Does a good Irishman give up the traditional corned beef and cabbage with a beer for Lent or not?

Every data warehouse will have a calendar table. Since everything has to exist in time, it is probably the most general dimension in a data warehouse. Since most data warehouses store only a few years of data at most, the calendar table does not have to have many rows (unless the granularity is in seconds—Wal-Mart may want to track trends by time of day).

However, it can be wide, because it has to also contain information about holidays, workdays, fiscal calendars, day of the week, Julianized days, and many other things. All SQL products have some built-in temporal functions that can extract the year, month, and day from a date; do simple temporal math; and so forth; but joins are easier to optimize when they do not involve function calls.

3.3.1　Report Range Tables

Another common form of temporal table is based on date ranges, which may or may not overlap. They are used for reports based on such things as seasons, promotions, and weather conditions. Such things might be reoccurring, like the seasons of the year or fixed holidays. However, they can also be a one-time event, like a sales promotion.

```
CREATE TABLE ReportRanges
(report_name CHAR(20) NOT NULL PRIMARY KEY,
 start_date DATE NOT NULL,
 end_date DATE NOT NULL,
 CHECK (start_date <= end_date,
  --other data
);
```

You should consider using a superkey made up of (report_name, start_date) or of (report_name, start_date, end_date) to get a covering index to speed up searching.

You might build several of these range tables for various purposes. Fiscal calendar reporting will be different from shopping seasons (e.g., Christmas or Easter) and would probably not be used at the same time. Fiscal calendars will not have overlaps, while promotions very well might. For example, the 4th of July might occur in the middle of our annual "Bikini Madness Sale."

```
INSERT INTO PromoReports
VALUES ('4-th of July-2006', '2006-07-04', '2006-07-04',
..),
     ('Bikini Madness-2006' '2006-07-01', '2006-07-15',
..);
```

If you have set up the start and end dates of the range properly, then you can use a simple BETWEEN predicate to get the data. It is also handy to have the year (or other granularity) as part of the report name, so it can be unique.

Here are the common templates for most queries:

1.　　Which promotional events were in effect on a particular date?

```
SELECT P.report_name
```

```
      FROM PromoReports AS P
      WHERE :my_date BETWEEN P.start_date AND P.end_date;
```

Use these queries inside IN() predicates against the fact table.

2.   When was that promotional event in effect? Notice that this version will give you all of the years in the fact table.

```
      SELECT :my_pormo, P.start_date, P.end_date
        FROM PromoReports AS P
       WHERE P.promo_name LIKE :my_promo ||'%';
```

If your postfix on the report name has a known pattern, then use "?" wild cards and explicit punctuation characters instead of "%" to get a bit more speed.

3.4   Helper Tables

This term comes from Ralph Kimball, so even if we had a better term, nobody would use it. These tables sit between the fact table and a dimension table to hold sets of dimensional values under a single name for the fact table. (This resolves M:M relationships between facts and dimensions—which is an issue for the star-schema pattern.) We will discuss this idea in detail in Chapter 13.

For example, when you go to a doctor, you get a bill for the visit. That single visit could have one or more International Classification of Disease (ICD) codes in the diagnosis.

The first option for recordkeeping is to keep only the primary diagnosis. This is usually what the doctors treat; other diagnoses are ignored until they are handled. In this example, this approach has merit. However, you are losing data.

The next option is to add more columns for the primary and secondary diagnoses out to some fixed limit. Most medical systems do not go beyond three codes. I have to hope that I do not have a lot of people who have more diseases than my limit. You will need to be sure the same ICD does not appear twice, that they are properly ordered (i.e., cancer is more important than acne), and so forth.

But what if the fact table really has a multivalued attribute of unknown size? Let's say I am keeping a data warehouse on a Chinese restaurant at the sales-ticket level. Each sale can have many items and probably will. I have my entrée dimension. I have my sales fact table. But in between them, I need a helper table:

```
CREATE TABLE TakeoutHelper
(salesticket_nbr INTEGER NOT NULL
   REFERENCES Sales(salesticket_nbr),
 entree_code INTEGER NOT NULL
    REFERENCES Entrees(entree_code),
 PRIMARY KEY (takeout_nbr, entree_code));
```

In the case of my Chinese restaurant, I will have a pattern on the take-out orders because of the rules for ordering—pick one item from column A and one from column B. So I could use this knowledge to initially load the helper table. But over time, someone will want a combination that does not appear on the menu.

The helper table will have to be adjusted when new combinations show up. It is probably a good idea to do this when you are scrubbing the data before inserting it into the data warehouse. Again, see Chapter 13 for the SQL needed to do this kind of classification.

3.5 Surrogate Keys

Ask about the internal implementation in your data warehouse product. The systems that are designed for this kind of work will create true surrogate keys. A common programming method is to build your own "quasi-surrogate keys" by using a proprietary autonumbering feature in a particular SQL engine. This is a good sign that you are not using a SQL product meant for data warehousing. The system should be doing this kind of thing under the covers for you.

The early SQL products were built on existing file systems. The data was kept in physically contiguous disk pages, in physically contiguous rows, made up of physically contiguous columns. In short, this was just like a deck of punch cards or a magnetic tape. Most programmers still carry that mental model, which is why I keep doing this rant.

Can you explain from a logical model why the same rows in the second query get different IDENTITY numbers? In the relational model, they should be treated the same if all the values of all the attributes are identical.

Using IDENTITY as a primary key is a sign that there is no data model, only an imitation of a sequential file system. Since this "magic, all-purpose, one-size-fits-all" pseudo-identifier exists only as a result of the physical state of a particular piece of hardware at a particular time as read by the current release of a particular database product, how do you verify that an entity has such a number in the reality you are modeling?

A quote from Dr. Codd: "Database users may cause the system to generate or delete a surrogate, but they have no control over its value, nor is its value ever displayed to them . . ." (Dr. Codd in *ACM TODS*, pp. 409–410) and Codd, E. (1979), Extending the Database Relational Model to Capture More Meaning. *ACM Transactions on Database Systems*, 4(4): 397–434.

This means that a surrogate ought to act like an index—created by the user, managed by the system, and *never* seen by a user. That means never in queries or anything else that a user does.

Codd also wrote the following:

> There are three difficulties in employing user-controlled keys as permanent surrogates for entities.
>
> (1) The actual values of user-controlled keys are determined by users and must therefore be subject to change by them (e.g. if two companies merge, the two employee databases might be combined with the result that some or all of the serial numbers might be changed).
>
> (2) Two relations may have user-controlled keys defined on distinct domains (e.g. one uses Social Security, while the other uses employee serial numbers) and yet the entities denoted are the same.
>
> (3) It may be necessary to carry information about an entity either before it has been assigned a user-controlled key value or after it has ceased to have one (e.g. an applicant for a job and a retiree).
>
> These difficulties have the important consequence that an equi-join on common key values may not yield the same result as a join on common entities. A solution . . . is to introduce entity domains that contain system-assigned surrogates. Database users may cause the system to generate or delete a surrogate, but they have no control over its value, nor is its value ever displayed to them... (E. Codd in *ACM TODS*, pp. 409–410).

3.6 Degenerate Dimensions

A degenerate dimension is a value in the fact table that has no dimensional tables to reference. These are usually keys of some sort, such as the sales ticket numbers on purchases, credit card numbers, and so forth. There is no meaningful way to put them into a category or hierarchy scheme for reporting; they are complete within themselves.

Besides their guarantee of uniqueness, groupings are possible in the fact table. A sales ticket number would tie all the items in a single purchase together so I can analyze the purchase as a whole. A credit card number gives me an idea of how much time and money a customer spends with my company.

The first trick is to determine when a dimension is degenerate or just useless. A comment column in the OLTP data is probably not worth putting in a fact table in the data warehouse. What could you do with it?

Next, does the dimension change over time, so that we need to either keep a history in a dimension or to bring old data up to the new format? A good example of this was a switch from one point of sale (POS) system to a new one, which handled the sale ticket number differently. The new format was longer, but it was fairly easy to convert the old data by adding a few characters to it.

While most of the work could be done by computer, the mappings to LLC classes D (History), J (Political Science), and K (Law) are still in process; the work is being done by subject matter experts who have to co-ordinate with international standards organizations.

CHAPTER 4

Data Migration and Scrubbing

THIS CHAPTER IS based on a white paper I wrote for Sunopsis (www.sunopsis.com) in 2005 and an article at DBAzine.com (http://www.dbazine.com/ofinterest/oi-articles/celko19 http://www.dbazine.com/ofinterest/oi-articles/celko20 http://www.dbazine.com/ofinterest/oi-articles/celko21). First, let me speak two simple truths that we all know about the environment in which our data lives.

The first truth is that no enterprise runs on one and only one database or data source today. Any enterprise of medium to large size will have desktop databases, department-level servers, enterprise-level servers, and data warehouse servers. If you do not have different platforms, then you are doing something wrong. While virtually all databases today run some version of SQL, they do not implement it in the same way. The same hardware and software that runs a data warehouse would be overkill for a departmental server doing OLTP.

The second truth is that no enterprise database is isolated. The connections between your enterprise and the rest of the world are now database to database, or service to service—no longer existing only on paper forms. Orders to suppliers, shipments to customers, and any other business activities require that your database application talks to someone else's database application. Payments are made and accepted through your bank, PayPal, or other commercial services. Shipping is done via UPS, Fed Ex, DHL, and the other delivery companies; you track your merchandise by accessing their database applications, not by building your own.

Passive data sources are now a commodity. It would be insane to try to maintain your own postal code database when you can buy the data from the U.S. Postal Service for a few dollars. Likewise, you would use the UPC barcodes that come on packaging instead of inventing your own encoding scheme and printing labels.

The small enterprise often has an arrogant feeling that it can ignore external data sources. The truth is that small enterprises are actually more vulnerable than the larger companies. Small- to medium-sized enterprises cannot afford the personnel, time, and resources to verify and validate data like a large enterprise can. They often leave the data in the format they got it. The result is "islands of data" that communicate with spreadsheets and homemade data transfer solutions.

4.1 Pumping Data

We have been transferring data with tools for a long time now. We have always written small routines in C or assembly language to convert EBCDIC to ASCII, to shift from lower- to uppercase, perhaps do simple math, table lookups, and so forth.

These early creatures did one transformation in one direction and required a reasonably skilled programmer to write them. Any change in the target or the source files meant rewriting the code. As the number of file formats increased, this was simply not a workable approach; a mere five file formats meant 50 routines.

By the 1980s, these programs evolved into the early file transfer products, usually designed to move data between mainframes and smaller systems. There was a user interface, and you did not have to be much of a programmer to use these products. The usual approach was to convert the source data into an intermediate format and then into the target format.

The raw speed of custom, low-level programming was traded for more flexible interfaces. Some of the products also began adding a simple programming language, usually some kind of BASIC interpreter, so some of the transforms could be customized. These are still very simple creatures.

A new creature appeared in the environment in the 1970s—the databases. The idea was that the enterprise could have one central repository for its data. It would be a trusted source; it would remove redundancy; and the DBMS (Database Management System) could enforce some of the data integrity rules. After a fairly brief period, proprietary navigational databases lost out to SQL databases. While there are many SQL dialects, the language is standardized enough that a programmer can quickly learn a new dialect. But this also meant that the programmers had to learn to think in a more abstract model of data instead of the more physical file model.

File systems are nothing like SQL databases. Rows are not records. A record is defined in the application program that reads it; a row is defined in the database schema and not by a program at all. In a record-based application, the name of the field comes from the application program in the READ, INPUT, or DATA DIVISION statements.

Compare this to a database. A row is named, defined, and constrained in the database schema, apart from any applications that might use it. A database actively seeks to maintain the correctness of all its data. Columns have strong data types. Constraints in the data declaration language (DDL) prevent incorrect data. Declarative referential integrity (DRI) says, in effect, that data in one table has a particular relationship with data in a second (possibly the same) table. It is also possible to have the database change itself via referential actions associated with the DRI actions and triggers.

4.2   Verification and Validation

All this means that when you move data into an RDBMS, you no longer have to write code to do all the data verification and validation in a low-level language that used to be needed to protect yourself when you wrote homemade transfer routines or used simple file transfer products.

Another simple truth that everyone knows but will not admit is that we never actually did much verification and validation in a low-level language when we custom built transfer routines. Some of the most spectacular data quality failures were the result of blindly loading data into files. Suddenly, you can find that you have absurd values and nonexistent codes in the data.

My personal favorite was a major credit card company that bought public record data that had been misaligned by one punch card column so that the letter "d" at the end of a town name fell into a status field. The "d" stood for "deceased" and all of the holders of the credit card from that town had their cards canceled in one day.

4.3   Extract, Transform, and Load (ETL)

The file transfer products continued to evolve and became *extract, transform, and load* (ETL) products aimed at the new databases. They added fancier "mousey-click" user interfaces, libraries of functions that could be combined via that interface, and fancier custom programming languages.

But they never got over their heritage. The intermediate file format became XML or another markup language. The proprietary ETL programming languages started to look more like Java and C++ than BASIC. But the underlying model for the conversion remained a one-record-at-a-time pipeline from source to target.

The connection to a database is typically ODBC (Open DataBase Connectivity), JDBC (Java DataBase Connectivity), or another session connection. Some ETL products can take advantage of bulk-loading utility programs if the data is staged to a file. At this point, the ETL products have become complex enough to require special training and certification in their proprietary language and various options. A mixed environment can be a problem to maintain and might conflict with bulk-load utilities from the vendor.

4.4   Databases Also Evolved

The relational model has some implications. There is a separation between the abstraction and the physical models. A set model of data is naturally parallel, while a file is naturally sequential. There is no requirement for rows to be implemented as physically contiguous fields in files of physically contiguous records.

A declarative programming language like SQL lets a programmer tell the database engine what he or she wants and leaves it to the optimizer to figure out how to do it. There is no one, single way to implement the logical model in hardware or software.

As a result, no two SQL engines are structurally alike internally, because they've all found niches in the ecology. Some are built for OLTP, some for OLAP, and some are for VLDB. They all will accept SQL but execute it totally differently.

The general standardized interfaces like ODBC or JDBC still exist and have their places. But the RDBMS products also evolved their own routines for moving and inserting data directly in their different architectures. These utility programs have an advantage over the external ETL packages, since they are targeted at the particular underlying architecture and can take advantage of the SQL engine.

However, the utility programs are limited and could not be used for complex transformations. The reason that you want to get the full power of SQL is that yet another creature suddenly appeared—the data warehouses.

4.5   Data Warehouses

The database servers also evolved, becoming bigger, faster, and more parallel. When the cost of storage plummeted below a certain point, it became possible to build data warehouses. A data warehouse is a large database that holds huge amounts of historical data for analysis. Data warehouses are not like OLTP databases. In fact, they are almost point for point the opposite, as I outlined at the start of this book.

The poor SQL programmer who has grown up in the OLTP world is suddenly as helpless in the data warehouse world as the traditional programmer who was dropped into a nonprocedural SQL world. Now we have Java programmers, but that's another story.

The next step in the evolution is to do the data transformations inside the databases themselves. Talk to any SQL programmer, and you will find that this is not a radical new idea but a common practice that needs to be automated. SQL programmers have been creating staging or working tables to bring data into their schemas for years.

The reasons for such ad hoc techniques are that SQL programmers know SQL. There is no need to pull up a special tool and learn it for simple jobs. However, the SQL-86 and SQL-89 standards defined a language too weak to replace the ETL tools, so code generation for data transformation was not possible.

Thank goodness everything keeps evolving, including SQL. Most of the SQL-92 standard and parts of the SQL-99 standard are common in all major products today. The addition of the CASE expression, OUTER JOINs, temporal functions, row constructors, common table expressions (CTE), and OLAP functions makes the language complete enough to do any extractions and transformations required.

Every SQL product has a stored procedure mechanism, so we started saving these scrubbing and data transforms. When we did these ad hoc SQL routines, we noticed that they ran faster than external ETL routines. There was also a certain sense of safety, knowing that the SQL is using one and only one set of rules for rounding, truncation, math, and string handling.

Database vendors also entered the ETL market with products like Oracle's Warehouse Builder, IBM's Warehouse Manager, and Microsoft's

DTS for SQL Server. These tools are built with one vendor's SQL engine internals. These tools are cheap or free with the database and will probably cut into the traditional ETL tool market. However, we are back to the original problem. You have to learn the proprietary languages and conventions of the vendor's ETL tool.

4.6 Extract, Load, and then Transform (E-L-T)

Proprietary ETL tools have difficulties keeping up with vendor SQL products. Any change in one SQL product has to be reflected in the proprietary tool, but without changing the proprietary language and interface.

In the meantime, the SQL vendors have been adding their own data migration tools to their offerings to compete with the ETL providers. But they tune their tools for their databases and generic connections like JDBC, ODBC, and so forth. So you needed to get all the SQL guys together to write and tune the interfaces.

What we really need is a way to centralize control, relocate code, or establish connections among the databases involved. We are working at too low a level for the problem, and nobody is going to be a current expert in dozens of SQL products.

Enter Sunopsis and their *extract, load, and then transform* (E-L-T) approach. Sunopsis will generate native SQL code or generic SQL on any of the over 50 different RDBMS that it handles. Sunopsis is written in Java, so will run on any platform, from mainframe to desktop. A user without in-depth SQL experience can sit at the graphic interface and connect "boxes and pipes" to set up a flow of data from one part of the enterprise to another. The code is generated and compiled automatically.

This is flexible and very quick. For example, if I decide that I want a transformation routine moved from its own stand-alone server system to a large VLDB system to improve performance, I simply drag the icon to the VLDB system from the hub server system. Sunopsis will do the work to set up the connections and will create the local SQL. In many cases, you will get two to three orders of magnitude improvement in performance over a traditional ETL tool sitting on a hub server. This is especially true in the case of parallelism in VLDB products.

But the real strength of Sunopsis is the ability to add your own SQL code generation to the repository. You can target the features of each RDBMS if you have an experienced programmer in that product. The system will maintain the code and can track the scripts, so that if you improve a routine, all the scripts that used the original version will update the new version.

4.6.1   Does It Work?

The real question is: How well does this generated code work? Obviously this is not a simple question, and results will vary. But we can get a sense of the power of the generated code with two examples from a real-life customer on a 12-node Teradata v2R5 database.

The first example is a simple join and aggregation process. One table of approximately 37.2 million rows is inner joined to a second table of approximately 19.2 million on two columns, and a MAX() is computed on a third column. This is a common insertion problem in a data warehouse and shows what bulk insertion can be like.

```
Number of rows inserted: 18,533,841
Elapsed: 2 min 7 sec
Rows/sec: 145,936
```

The second example is a complex data warehouse snapshot query. A central fact table is outer joined to a dozen dimensional tables. The approximate table sizes and the kinds of joins are given next.

Fact table = 18.2 million rows

Table 1 < 1,000 rows inner join on one column

Table 2 < 1,000 rows inner join on one column

Table 3 = 18.5 million rows, left outer join on two columns

Table 4 = 15.9 million rows, left outer join on two columns

Table 5 = 6.7 million rows, left outer join on two columns

Table 6 = 1 million rows, left outer join on two columns

Table 7 = 1 million rows, left outer join on two columns

Table 8 = 18.2 million rows, left outer join on two columns

Table 9 = 3,000 rows, left outer join on two columns

Table 10 = 28,000 rows, left outer join on three columns

Table 11 = 15.7 million rows, left outer join on two columns

Table 12 = 1.5 Million rows, left outer join on two columns

```
Number of rows inserted: 18,207,198
Elapsed: 6 min 47 sec
Rows/sec: 44,735
```

I think that anyone who has done a job like this will agree that this query is a good "stress test" for any kind of data transfer operation.

4.7 Scrubbing Data with Non-First-Normal-Form (1NF) Tables

We can do this kind of coding by hand, though I do not recommend it for serious production work. However, it is a good idea to know how to do it when you don't have code generator tools.

4.7.1 Setting up a Scrubbing Table

SQL does not require that a table have unique constraints, a primary key, or anything else that would ensure data integrity. In short, you can use a table pretty much like a file if you wish. Is this a bad thing?

Well, mostly yes and a little no. You should never have such a beast in your final OLTP schema, but one common programming trick is to use a table without any constraints as a staging area. You load data from an external source into one of these non-TABLEs, scrub it, and pass it along to a real table in the actual schema. The trouble is that a lot of the time, the non-TABLE is denormalized and full of bad data. You can do some normalization from the staging table into another set of scrubbing tables, but you can also do some work with the table as it stands.

This example is based on material posted by a newbie on a SQL newsgroup, but this situation is not uncommon. The newbie gets raw data from a source that can have duplicate rows and repeating groups in violation of first normal form (1NF). The scrub tables look like this:

```
CREATE TABLE PeopleSkills
(name VARCHAR(10) NOT NULL,
  code1 INTEGER NOT NULL,
  code2 INTEGER NOT NULL,
  code3 INTEGER NOT NULL,
  code4 INTEGER NOT NULL,
  code5 INTEGER NOT NULL);

INSERT INTO PeopleSkills VALUES ('Mary', 1, 7, 8, 9, 13);
INSERT INTO PeopleSkills VALUES ('Mary', 1, 7, 8, 9, 13);
INSERT INTO PeopleSkills VALUES ('Mary', 1, 7, 7, 7, 13);
```

```
INSERT INTO PeopleSkills VALUES ('Mary', 1, 7, 8, 9, 13);
INSERT INTO PeopleSkills VALUES ('Joe', 1, 7, 8, 9, 3);
INSERT INTO PeopleSkills VALUES ('Bob', 1, 7, 8, 9, 3);
INSERT INTO PeopleSkills VALUES ('Larry', 22, 17, 18, 19, 113);
-- no target codes
INSERT INTO PeopleSkills VALUES ('Mary', 1, 3, 2, 9, 13);
INSERT INTO PeopleSkills VALUES ('Melvin', 1, 3, 2, 9, 13);
-- 2 target codes
INSERT INTO PeopleSkills VALUES ('Irving', 1, 8, 2, 9, 13);
-- 1 targetcodes
```

Part of the scrubbing is to find out which people have some or all of a particular code. The list can change, so we put it in a table of its own, like this:

```
CREATE TABLE TargetCodes
(code INTEGER NOT NULL PRIMARY KEY,
 description VARCHAR(50) NOT NULL);
INSERT INTO TargetCodes
VALUES (1, 'code1'), (3, 'code3'), (7, 'code7');
```

The first goal is to return a report with the names of the people and the number of target codes they have in their skills inventory. The first thought of an experienced SQL programmer is to normalize the repeated group. The obvious way to do this is with a derived table, thus:

```
SELECT P1.name, COUNT(*)
  FROM (SELECT name, code1 FROM PeopleSkills
         UNION
         SELECT name, code2 FROM PeopleSkills
         UNION
         SELECT name, code3 FROM PeopleSkills
         UNION
         SELECT name, code4 FROM PeopleSkills
         UNION
         SELECT name, code5 FROM PeopleSkills)
         AS P1 (name, code) -- normalized table!
       LEFT OUTER JOIN
       TargetCodes AS T1
       ON T1.code = P1.code
  GROUP BY P1.name;
```

The reason that this fool experienced SQL programmers is that they know that a schema should be in 1NF format, and they immediately fix that problem without looking a bit further. They want to correct the design problem first. That chain of UNIONs can be replaced by a chain of ORs, hidden in an IN() predicate. This one is not so bad to write:

```
SELECT P1.name, COUNT (DISTINCT T1.code) AS tally
   FROM PeopleSkills AS P1
        LEFT OUTER JOIN
        TargetCodes AS T1
        ON T1.code IN (code1, code2, code3, code4, code5)
GROUP BY name;
```

```
Results
name     tally
==============
'Bob'        3
'Irving'     1
'Joe'        3
'Larry'      0
'Mary'       3
'Melvin'     2
```

The trick is the use of an IN() predicate when you have a repeating group. This will give you just the names of those who have one or more target codes.

```
SELECT DISTINCT name
   FROM PeopleSkills AS P1
WHERE code1 IN (SELECT code FROM TargetCodes)
   OR code2 IN (SELECT code FROM TargetCodes)
   OR code3 IN (SELECT code FROM TargetCodes)
   OR code4 IN (SELECT code FROM TargetCodes)
   OR code5 IN (SELECT code FROM TargetCodes);
```

This next modification will show you which codes each person has, with 1/0 flags. This has a neat trick with the little-used SUM(DISTINCT <exp>) construction, but you have to know what the target codes are in advance.

```
SELECT name,
       SUM(DISTINCT
           CASE WHEN 1 IN (code1, code2, code3, code4, code5)
                THEN 1 ELSE 0 END) AS code1,
       SUM(DISTINCT
           CASE WHEN 3 IN (code1, code2, code3, code4, code5)
                THEN 1 ELSE 0 END) AS code3,
       SUM(DISTINCT
           CASE WHEN 7 IN (code1, code2, code3, code4, code5)
                THEN 1 ELSE 0 END) AS code7
  FROM PeopleSkills AS P1
GROUP BY name;
```

Results

Name	code1	code3	code7
'Bob'	1	1	1
'Irving'	1	0	0
'Joe'	1	1	1
'Larry'	0	0	0
'Mary'	1	1	1
'Melvin'	1	1	0

Another trick for scrubbing such data is the Bose-Nelson sort (R. C. Bose and R. J. Nelson, "A Sorting Problem," *Journal of the ACM*, 9, pp. 282–296, and my article in *Dr. Dobb's Journal* back in 1985(Bose-Nelson Sort (DR. DOBBS JOURNAL, 1985 Sep, M&T Publications, now Miller-Freeman). This is a recursive procedure that takes an integer and then generates swap pairs for a vector of that size. A swap pair is a pair of position numbers from 1 to (n) in the vector that need to be exchanged if they are out of order. Swap pairs are also related to sorting networks in the literature (see Donald Knuth, *The Art of Computer Programming* Volumes 1-3 Boxed Set by Donald E. Knuth (September 1998, ISBN: 0-201-48541-9, Addison-Wesley).

You are probably thinking that this method is a bit weak, because the results are only good for sorting a fixed number of items. But a table only has a fixed number of columns, so that is not a problem in denormalized SQL.

You can set up a sorting network that will sort five items, with the minimal number of exchanges, nine swaps, like this:

```
swap (c1, c2);
swap (c4, c5);
swap (c3, c5);
swap (c3, c4);
swap (c1, c4);
swap (c1, c3);
swap (c2, c5);
swap (c2, c4);
swap (c2, c3);
```

You might want to deal yourself a hand of five playing cards in one suit to see how it works. Put the cards face down on the table and pick up the pairs, swapping them if required, then turn over the row to see that it is in sorted order when you are done.

In theory, the minimum number of swaps needed to sort (n) items is CEILING(log2 (n!)), and, as (n) increases, this approaches O(n*log2(n)). Computer science majors will remember the "Big O" expression as the expected performance of the best sorting algorithms, such as Quicksort. The Bose-Nelson method is very good for small values of (n). If (n < 9), then it is perfect, actually. But as things get bigger, Bose-Nelson approaches O(n ^ 1.585). In English, this method is good for a fixed-size list of 16 or fewer items and goes to hell after that.

You can write a version of the Bose-Nelson procedure that will output the SQL code for a given value of (n). The obvious direct way to do a swap(x, y) is to write a chain of UPDATE statements. Remember that in SQL, the SET clause assignments happen in parallel, so you can easily write a SET clause that exchanges the two items when they are out of order. Using the previous swap chain, we get this block of code:

```
BEGIN ATOMIC
-- swap (code1, code2);
UPDATE PeopleSkills
   SET code1 = code2, code2 = code1
 WHERE code1 > code2;

-- swap (code4, code5);
UPDATE PeopleSkills
   SET code4 = code5, code5 = code4
WHERE code4 > code5;

-- swap (code3, code5);
```

```
UPDATE PeopleSkills
   SET code3 = code5, code5 = code3
 WHERE code3 > code5;


-- swap (code3, code4);
UPDATE PeopleSkills
   SET code3 = code4, code4 = code3
 WHERE code3 > code4;


-- swap (code1, code4);
UPDATE PeopleSkills
   SET code1 = code4, code4 = code1
 WHERE code1 > code4;


-- swap (code1, code3);
UPDATE PeopleSkills
   SET code1 = code3, code3 = code1
 WHERE code1 > code3;


-- swap (code2, code5);
UPDATE PeopleSkills
   SET code2 = code5, code5 = code2
 WHERE code2 > code5;


-- swap (code2, code4);
UPDATE PeopleSkills
   SET code2 = code4, code4 = code2
 WHERE code2 > code4;


-- swap (code2, code3);
UPDATE PeopleSkills
   SET code2 = code3, code3 = code2
 WHERE code2 > code3;

SELECT * FROM PeopleSkills;
END;
```

This is fully portable, standard SQL code, and it can be machine generated. But that parallelism is useful. It is worthwhile to combine some of the UPDATE statements, but you have to be careful not to change the effective sequence of the swap operations.

If you look at the first two UPDATE statements, you can see that they do not overlap. This means you could roll them into one statement like this:

```
-- swap (code1, code2) AND swap (code4, code5);

UPDATE Foobar
   SET code1 = CASE WHEN code1 <= code2 THEN code1 ELSE code2
END,
       code2 = CASE WHEN code1 <= code2 THEN code2 ELSE code1
END,
       code4 = CASE WHEN code4 <= code5 THEN code4 ELSE code5
END,
       code5 = CASE WHEN code4 <= code5 THEN code5 ELSE code4 END
 WHERE code4 > code5 OR code1 > code2;
```

The advantage of doing this is that you have to execute only one UPDATE statement, rather than two. Updating a table, even on nonkey columns, usually locks the table and prevents other users from getting to the data. If you could roll the statements into one single UPDATE, you would have the best of all possible worlds, but I doubt that the code would be easy to read. I'll leave that as an exercise to the reader.

4.7.2   Designing a Target Table

In section 4.7.1, we wrote queries for getting data from a non-first-normal-form (NFNF or non-1NF) table. Let's assume that you are moving data from a file into such a table. What should the target table look like?

The usual answer is to make all the columns NVARCHAR(n), where (n) is the maximum size allowed by your particular SQL product. This is the most general data type, and it can hold all kinds of garbage. The real shame about this schema design is that people do use it in their OLTP database—and not just as a staging area for scrubbing bad data. For the record, these are quick and dirty tricks for data scrubbing when you don't have any other tools. If you do have data scrubbing tools, use them instead.

The first question to ask is whether you should be using NVARCHAR(n) or simply VARCHAR(n)? If you allow a national character set, you can catch some errors that might not be seen in a simple Latin-1 alphabet. But most of the time, you can be sure that the file was in ASCII or EBCDIC by the time you moved it to the staging table with a utility program, such as the BCP (Bulk Copy Program) utility in the SQL server family.

The quick way to do this is with a comma-separated values (CSV) file. You can modify such a file with a text editor. If worse comes to worst, you can even add individual "INSERT INTO <column list> VALUES (<csv string>);" code around each line and run the file as a SQL transaction with save points.

The second question is which value of (n) to use? Setting it to the max is fine for the first scrubbing. The next thing you are going to do is run a query that looks for the minimum, maximum, and average length of each of the columns. If a column is supposed to be a fixed length, then all three of these should be the same.

If a column is supposed to be of varying length, then all three of these should be in a reasonable range. How do you define reasonable? Bigger than zero length is often a good criterion for a column being too short. This can happen when a field was skipped on an input form or when errors were made in converting it into a CSV file. As a recent personal example, I moved an ACT file into SQL server using the ACT utility program to get a CSV file and found several rows where the data had gotten shifted over one position, leaving blank or empty columns.

You generally have some idea if a varying column is too long. For example, the U.S. Postal Service standards for labels use CHAR(35), so any address line longer than that is suspect (and cannot be used on bulk mailings).

If you have columns that are longer than expected, the first action should be to UPDATE the scrub table using TRIM() and REPLACE() functions to remove extra blanks. Extra white space is the usual culprit. You might find it is faster to do this quick cleanup in the original CSV file with a text editor.

However, other simple edits are probably best done in SQL, since a text editor does not see the individual fields. You might want to change "Street" to "St" to keep mailing addresses short, but a text editor will cheerfully make "John Longstreet" into "John Longst" as well.

In the same UPDATE, you can use UPPER() or LOWER() to be sure that your data is in the right case. Proper capitalization for text is a bit harder, and if you have to do this often, it is a good idea to write a stored procedure or user-defined function in the 4GL language that came with your SQL product.

Finally, look at the data itself. Many SQL products offer functions that test to see if a string is a valid numeric expression or to cast it into a numeric. But you have to be careful, since some of these functions stop parsing as soon as they have a numeric string; that is, given the string "123XX," your library function might return 123 and ignore the invalid characters at the end.

Most SQL products have some kind of regular expression predicate that works like the SQL-92 SIMILAR TO predicate or the grep() utilities in UNIX. This is a great tool for validating the scrubbed data, but it has some limits. It tells you only that the data is in a validate format, but not if it is valid data.

For example, given a date of "12/11/03" you have no idea if it was supposed to be "2003-11-12" or "2003-12-11" without outside information. This is why we have the ISO-8601 standards for displaying temporal data. Likewise "2003-02-30" will pass a simple regular expression parse, but there is no such date.

One of the most common errors in file systems was to load the same raw data into the file more than once. Sometimes it was literally the same data—an operator hung a magnetic tape, loaded a file, and then forgot to mark the job as having been done. The next shift came to work and repeated the operation. Other times, a data entry clerk simply input the same data twice or sent a correction without removing the erroneous data. Given an impatient user with a fast mouse button, you can create the same problem in a new technology.

At this point, you are ready to move the raw data to a new table with columns that have appropriate data types but no constraints just yet. The move should be done with an "INSERT INTO ... SELECT DISTINCT ... " to get rid of the redundant duplicates.

4.7.3   Adding Constraints and Validations

At this point, the data has been scrubbed a bit and moved to a table with the correct data types but no constraints or validations on the columns.

There is a temptation to simply load it into the "real tables" in the database. Resist the temptation. The syntax of the data might be acceptable, but that does not mean the data itself is right.

We can classify errors as single-column or multiple-column errors. A single-column error might be a gender code of "B" when only "M" or "F" is allowed. A multiple-column error involves individual columns that are valid, but the combination of which is invalid. For example, pregnancy is a valid medical condition, and male is a valid gender; however, a pregnant male is an invalid combination.

The first test is to see if your key is actually a key by running a test for NULLs and counting the occurrences of unique values:

```
SELECT key_1, key_2, ...  key_n
  FROM ScrubTank
 GROUP BY key_1, key_2, ...  key_n
HAVING COUNT(*) > 1 -- dups
    OR (SIGN(key_1) + .. + SIGN(key_n) IS NULL
```

You can also use SUBSTRING(), CASE, or other functions with concatenation so that any NULL will propagate.

Let's assume we have a column with a code that is five characters long, and we have trimmed and edited the original raw data until all the rows of that column are indeed CHAR(5). But there is a syntax rule that the code is of this format (using SQL-99 predicates):

```
CHECK (Foo_code SIMILAR TO
'[:UPPER:][:UPPER:][:DIGIT:][:DIGIT:][:DIGIT:]')
```

If you add this to your scrub table with an ALTER TABLE statement, you need to know whether your SQL product will immediately test existing data for compatibility or whether the constraint will go into effect only for inserted or updated data.

Instead of adding the check constraints all at once, write case expressions that will do the testing for you. The format is simple and can be done with a text editor. Pull off the predicates from the CHECK()constraints in the target table and put them into a query like this:

```
SELECT
  CASE WHEN NOT <> THEN 'err_###'
       WHEN NOT <> THEN 'err_###'
       ...
       ELSE '  ' END AS <>,
  ...
  FROM ScrubTank;
```

A CASE expression will test each WHEN clause in the order written, so when you see one error message, you will need to correct it and then pass the data through the query again. The goal is to get a query with all blanks in the columns to show that all the rows have passed.

Rules that apply to more than one column can be tested with another query that looks for the table constraints in the same way. It is a good idea to do this as a separate step after the single-column validations. A correction in one column will often fix the multiple-column errors, too.

Hopefully, we are now ready to finally put the scrubbed data into one or more of the target tables in the actual database schema. This ought to be a simple "INSERT INTO.. SELECT.. FROM ScrubTank" statement.

Frankly, there are better tools for data scrubbing than pure SQL; this chapter was more of a "proof of concept" than a recommendation. If you have the logical constraints in the text of your database schema, then pulling them out is a matter of a text edit, rather than completely new programming. While this approach is a bit of work, it gives you a script that you can reuse and does not cost you any extra money for new software.

CHAPTER
5

MERGE Statement

IN THE 1950s, we would sort the transaction tape(s) and master tape on the same key, read each one looking for a match, and then perform whichever logic was needed. The output was a new master tape. This became the model for mainframe data processing until we got random access storage.

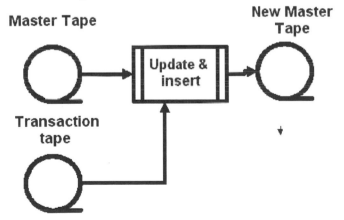

The SQL:2003 standard added a single statement to mimic a common magnetic tape file system "MERGE and insert" procedure. As more products add this feature, it will become more and more optimized and important for loading data in warehouses. It exists in

DB2, Oracle 10, and SQL Server 2005. The business logic, in a pseudo-code, looks like this:

```
FOR EACH row IN the Transactions table
DO IF working row NOT IN Master table
    THEN INSERT working row INTO the Master table;
    ELSE UPDATE Master table
            SET Master table columns to the Transactions table
values
            WHERE <matching criteria>;
    END IF;
END FOR;
```

The new MERGE statement attempts to imic this old logic, but it does not like the old procedural model. SQL is a declarative language, so a statement takes effect all at once, not in sequential steps.

5.1 Simple MERGE Statement

In its simplest form, the MERGE statement looks like this:

```
MERGE INTO <table name> [AS [<correlation name>]]
USING <table reference> ON <search condition>
{WHEN [NOT] MATCHED [AND <search condition>]
 THEN <modification operation>} ...
[ELSE IGNORE];
```

In effect, the <table name> would have been the master tape and the <table reference> would have been the transaction tape. You cannot use columns in the UPDATE SET clause that are specified in the ON condition. We do not want to "change the targets" on the fly. Unlike a magnetic tape, a SQL table is supposed to be updated all at once and not in sequence. The entire subset of rows to be updated must be selected, the entire set of rows to be inserted must be created, and the changes must be made all at once.

You will notice that use of a correlation name in the MERGE INTO clause is in complete violation of the principle that a correlation name effectively creates a temporary table that disappears at the end of the statement. There are several other places where SQL:2003 destroyed the original SQL language model, but you do not have to write irregular syntax in all cases.

After a row is matched (or not) to the target table, you can add more <search condition>s in the WHEN clauses. The <modification operation> clause can include insertion, update, or delete operations that follow the same rules as those single statements. This can hide complex programming logic in a single statement.

Let's assume that that we have a table of personnel salary changes at the branch office that is called PersonnelChanges. Here is a MERGE statement, which will take the contents of the PersonnelChanges table and MERGE them with a table called Personnel. Both of them use the emp_nbr as the key. Here is a typical, but very simple, use of MERGE INTO.

```
MERGE INTO Personnel AS P
USING (SELECT emp_nbr, salary, bonus, comm
         FROM PersonnelChanges) AS C
  ON P.emp_nbr = C.emp_nbr
WHEN MATCHED
THEN UPDATE
       SET (P.salary, P.bonus, P.comm)
           = (C.salary, C.bonus, C.comm)
WHEN NOT MATCHED
THEN INSERT(P.emp_nbr, P.salary, P.bonus, P.comm)
     VALUES(C.emp_nbr, C.salary, C.bonus,C.comm);
```

If you think about it for a minute, if there is a match, then all you can do is UPDATE the row. If there is no match, then all you can do is insert the new row.

There are proprietary versions of this statement and other options. In particular, look for the term "UPSERT" in the literature. These statements are most often used for adding data to a data warehouse.

5.2   Merging without the MERGE Statement

If you do not have this statement, you can get the same effect from this pseudocode block of code:

```
BEGIN ATOMIC
UPDATE T1
   SET (a, b, c, ..
        = (SELECT a, b, c, ..
             FROM T2
```

```
             WHERE T1.somekey = T2.somekey),
   WHERE EXISTS
          (SELECT *
             FROM T2
           WHERE T1.somekey = T2.somekey);

   INSERT INTO T1
   SELECT *
     FROM T2
    WHERE NOT EXISTS
          (SELECT *
             FROM T2
           WHERE T1.somekey = T2.somekey);
   END;
```

For performance, first do the UPDATE, then the INSERT INTO. If you INSERT INTO first, all rows just inserted will be scanned by the UPDATE as well.

5.3 TRIGGERs and MERGE

Let me deliver the punch line now and then prove my case:

1.   Do not use MERGE if you have statement-level triggers on a table.

2.   Do not write statement-level triggers if you use MERGE statement.

Having TRIGGERs of the tables in a MERGE are a bad idea. The MERGE is both an INSERT and UPDATE in one statement. When an INSERT statement inserts zero or more rows, it fires the BEFORE and AFTER insert triggers. Likewise, an UPDATE of zero or more rows fires those triggers as well. A set-oriented language considers an empty set to be a set.

MERGE is effectively doing two data manipulation language (DML) operations, but only one of them will actually affect (or create) a row. But it does this in the context of a single DML statement. However, n SQL statement is supposed to work "all at once"—not in a sequence of processing steps like the old tape MERGE algorithms. Should all the

BEFORE triggers fire first? Should all the AFTER triggers fire next? Should they be mixed?

The order of the triggers was clear when we had two separate DML statements. The MERGE fired the same triggers that the "UPDATE then INSERT" logic sequence fired. If the MERGE only executed the insert triggers because in the end it only did an insert, then it wouldn't be duplicating the "UPDATE then INSERT" concept.

I can write "UPDATE then INSERT" or "INSERT then UPDATE" procedural code. What if I switch the UPDATE and INSERT clause positions in the MERGE statement? Will that change the order of the TRIGGERs, like it would in the procedural code? That does not sound like desirable behavior for SQL.

5.4 Self-Referencing MERGE

There were both physical and logical reasons that the MERGE INTO <table name> and the USING <table reference> should not be the same. For example, we might pull out a subset of the Personnel table in the clause using an alias, change the data, and insert the rows back into the Personnel table, leaving the old rows in place. But what happened to the relational keys? A file system can have redundancy, because records are identified by physical location in storage rather than a relational key.

Since the table can be changed in different ways, depending on the order of execution and the TRIGGER problem, we now have the "timing" problem. In the original tape file merge and COBOL programming, the master file could not easily be backed up to look at a prior to or following a record on the tape. This is not true for a high-speed disk drive. Suddenly, I can try to update a row (which is nothing like a record!) to the same key or in violation of other constraints in the middle of the statement. This will force a ROLLBACK in the middle of the MERGE statement.

CHAPTER 6

OLAP Basics

OLAP USES A snapshot of a database taken at one point in time and then puts the data into a dimensional model. The purpose of this model is to run queries that deal with aggregations of data rather than individual transactions. In traditional file systems, we used indexes, hashing, and other tricks for the same purpose. We still have those tools, but we have added new ones. Star schemas, snowflake schemas, and multidimensional storage methods are all ways to get to the data faster.

6.1 Cubes

One such structure is the cube (or *hypercube*). Think of a two-dimensional cross-tabulation or a spreadsheet that models, say, a location (encoded as "North," "South," "East," and "West") and a product (encoded with category names). You have a grid that shows all possible combinations of locations and products, but many of the cells are going to be empty—you do not sell fur coats in the South or bikinis in the North.

Now extend the idea to more and more dimensions, such as "payment method," "coupons or not," and so forth; the grid becomes a cube, then a hypercube, and so forth. If you have trouble visualizing

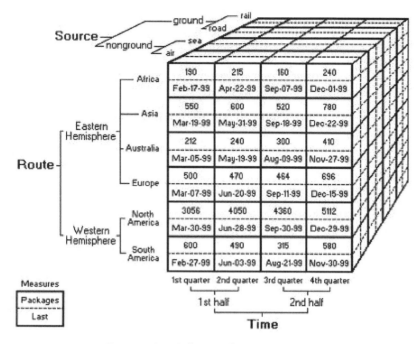

Figure 6.1 Cube in Three Dimensions

more than three dimensions, then imagine a control panel like you find on a stereo system. Each slider switch controls one aspect of the sound, such as balance, volume, bass, and treble. (See Figure 6.1.)

As you can see, actually materializing a cube would be very expensive, and most of the cells would be empty. Fortunately, we have prior experience with sparse arrays from scientific programming and a lot of database access methods.

The OLAP cube is created from a star schema of tables, which we'll discuss shortly. At the center is the fact table, which lists the core facts that make up the query. Basically, a star schema has a fact table that models the cells of a sparse array by linking them to dimension tables.

The real goal of the cube is to make aggregate calculations fast and easy. I want to be able to pick my dimensions and then pick the scales used to measure them.

6.2 Dr. Codd's OLAP Rules

Dr. E. F. Codd and associates published a white paper for Arbor Software (now Hyperion Solutions) in 1993, entitled "Providing OLAP (On-line Analytical Processing) to User-Analysts: An IT Mandate. (Arbor Software, 1993)" This paper introduced the term *OLAP* and a set of abstract rules somewhat like his rules for RDBMS. But because the paper had been sponsored by a commercial vendor (whose product matched those rules fairly well), rather than a pure research paper like his RDBMS work, it was not well received.

It was also charged that Dr. Codd himself allowed his name to be used and that he did not put much work into it, but let the vendor, his wife, and a research assistant do the work. The original white paper had 12 rules, and then added another 6 rules in 1995. The rules were restructured into four *feature groups*, which I will summarize here.

6.2.1 Basic Features

I am going to retain the original numbering, but add some more comments.

F1: *Multidimensional Conceptual View*. This means that data is kept in a matrix in which each dimension of the matrix is an attribute. This is a grid or spreadsheet model of data. This includes the ability to select subsets of data based on restrictions on the dimensions.

F2: *Intuitive Data Manipulation*. *Intuition* is a vague term that every vendor claims for its product. This is usually taken to mean that you have a graphical user interface (GUI) with the usual "drag-and-drop" feature and other graphic interfaces. This does not exclude a written programming language, but it does not give you any help with the design of it.

F3: *Accessibility: OLAP as a Mediator*. The OLAP engine is middleware between possibly heterogeneous data sources and an OLAP front end. You might want to compare this to the model for SQL, where the SQL engine sits between the user and the database.

F4: *Batch Extraction versus Interprtetive Extraction*. The OLAP has to have its own staging database for OLAP data as well as offer live access to external data. This is hybrid OLAP (HOLAP), which we will discuss shortly. Live access to external data is a serious problem, because it implies some kind of connection—and possibly huge and unexpected data flows into the staging database.

F5: *OLAP Analysis Models*. Dr. Codd described four analysis models in his white paper:

1. Categorical: Categorical models are the typical descriptive statistics we have seen in reports since the beginning of data processing.

2.   Exegetical: This model type is what we have been doing with spreadsheets—slice, dice, and drill down reporting on demand.

3.   Contemplative: This is a "what if?" analysis. There have been some specialized tools for doing this kind of modeling, and some of them use extensions to spreadsheet. Contemplative analysis lets you ask questions about the effects of changes on the whole system, such as, "What is the effect of closing the Alaska store to the company?" You have a particular idea you want to test.

4.   Formulaic: These are goal-seeking models. You know the outcome you want, but not how to get it. The model keeps changing parameters and doing the contemplations until it gets to the desired results (or proves that the goal is impossible). Here I would set a goal, such as, "How can I increase the sale of bikinis in the Alaska store?" and wait for an answer. The bad news is that there can be many solutions, no solution ("Bikinis in Alaska are doomed to failure"), or unacceptable solutions ("Close down all but the Alaska store").

Categorical and exegetical features are easy to implement. The contemplative and formulaic features are harder and more expensive to implement. We have some experience with formulaic and contemplative analysis with linear or constraint programming for industrial processes. However, the number of parameters is fairly small and very well controlled, while the results are measurable in well-defined units.

F6: *Client/Server Architecture*. This pretty well speaks for itself. The goal was to allow the users to share data easily and to be able to use any front-end tool.

F7: *Transparency*. This was part of the RDBMS model. The client front end should not have to be aware of how the connection to the OLAP engine or other data sources is made.

F8: *Multiuser Support*. This was also part of the RDBMS model. This is actually easy to, do because OLAP engines are read-only snapshots of data. There is no need for transaction controls for multiple users. However, a new breed of analytical database is designed to allow querying while data is being steamed from external data sources in real time.

6.2.2   Special Features

This feature list was added to make the OLAP engines practical.

F9: *Treatment of Nonnormalized Data*. This means we can load data from non-RDBMS sources. Part 9 of the SQL-99 standard also added the SQL management of external data (MED) feature for importing external data (CAN/CSA-ISO/IEC 9075-9-02 06-Mar-2003, adopted ISO/IEC 9075-9:2001, first edition, 2001-05-15). This proposal never got very far, but current ETL products can handle these transformations in their proprietary syntax.

F10: *Store OLAP Results*. This is a practical consideration. OLAP data is expensive, and you do not want to have to reconstruct it over and over from live data. The implication is that the OLAP database is a snapshot of the state of the data sources.

F11: *Extraction of Missing Values*. In his Relational Model Version 2 (RMV2), Codd defined two kinds of missing values rather than the single NULL used in SQL. One of them is similar to the SQL NULL, which models the attribute that exists in the entity, but we do not know its value. The second kind of missing value says that the attribute does not exist in the entity, so it will never have a value. Since most SQL products (the exception is First SQL) support only the first kind of NULL, it can be difficult to meet rule F11. However, there is some support in the CUBE and ROLLUP features for determining which NULLs were in the original data and which were created in the aggregation.

F12: *Treatment of Missing Values*. All missing values are ignored by the OLAP analyzer, regardless of their source. This follows the rules for dropping NULLs in aggregations in standard SQL.

6.2.3   Reporting Features

The reporting features are obviously the whole point of OLAP.

F13: *Flexible Reporting*. This feature is again a bit vague. Let's take it to mean that the dimensions can be aggregated and arranged pretty much any way the user wants to see the data. We will not be concerned with graphic displays versus text reports.

F14: *Uniform Reporting Performance*. Dr. Codd required that the reporting performance would not be significantly degraded by increasing the number of dimensions or database size. This is more of a product design goal than an abstract principle. If I have a precalculated database, the number of dimensions is not as much of a problem.

F15: *Automatic Adjustment of Physical Level*. Dr. Codd required that the OLAP system adjust its physical storage automatically. This can be done with utility programs in most products, so the user has some control over the adjustments.

6.2.4   Dimension Control

F16: *Generic Dimensionality*. Dr. Codd took the purist view that each dimension must be equivalent in both its structure and operational capabilities. This may not be unconnected with the fact that this is an Essbase characteristic. He did allow additional operational capabilities to be granted to selected dimensions (presumably including time), but he insisted that such additional functions should be grantable to any dimension. He did not want the basic data structures, formulas, or reporting formats to be biased toward any one dimension. This has proven to be one of the most controversial of all the original 12 rules. Technology-focused products tend to largely comply with it, so the vendors of such products support it. Application-focused products usually make no effort to comply, and their vendors bitterly attack the rule. With a strictly purist interpretation, few products fully comply. We would suggest that if you are purchasing a tool for general-purpose, multiple application use, then you want to consider this rule—but even then, give it a lower priority. If you are buying a product for a specific application, you may safely ignore the rule.

F17: *Unlimited Dimensions and Aggregation Levels*. This is physically impossible, so we can settle for a "large number" of dimensions and aggregation levels. Dr. Codd suggested that the product should support at least 15 and preferably 20 dimensions. The general rule is to have more than you need right now, so there is room for growth.

F18: *Unrestricted Cross-Dimensional Operations*. There is a difference between a calculation and an operation. Certain combinations of scales cannot be used in the same calculation to give a meaningful result (i.e., "What is Thursday divided by red?"). However, it is possible to do an operation on mixed data (i.e., "How many red shoes did we sell on Thursday?").

6.3   MOLAP

Multidimensional OLAP (MOLAP) is the "data in a grid" version that Dr. Codd described in his paper. This is where the idea of saving summary results first appeared. Generally speaking, MOLAP does fast simpler calculations on smaller databases. We have gotten very good with the design of spreadsheets over the last few decades, and that same technology can be used by MOLAP engines.

6.4 ROLAP

Relational OLAP (ROLAP) was developed after MOLAP. The main difference is that ROLAP does not do precomputation or store summary data in the database. ROLAP tools create dynamic SQL queries when the user requests the data. The exception to that description is the use of materialized VIEWs, which will persist summary data for queries that follow its first invocation. One goal of ROLAP was to be scalable, because of reduced storage requirements, and to be more flexible and portable because it uses SQL.

Another advantage is that the OLAP and transactional databases can be the same engine. RDBMS engines have gotten very good at handling large amounts of data, working in parallel, and optimizing queries stored in their particular internal formats. It is a shame to lose those advantages. For example, DB2's optimizer now detects a star schema by looking for a single large table with many smaller tables joined to it.

6.5 HOLAP

The problem with a pure ROLAP engine is that it is slower than MOLAP. Think about how most people actually work. A broad query is narrowed down to a more particular one. Particular tables, such as a general end-of the-month summary, can be constructed once and shared among many users.

This led to HOLAP, which retains some result tables in specialized storage or indexing, so that they can be reused. The base tables, dimension tables, and some summary tables are in the RDBMS. This is probably the most common approach in products today.

6.6 OLAP Query Languages

SQL is the standard query language for transactional databases. Other than a few OLAP features added to SQL-99, there is no such language for analytics. The closest thing is the MDX (Multi-Dimensional Expressions) language from Microsoft, which has become the de facto standard by virtue of Microsoft's market domination.

This is not because MDX is a technically brilliant language, but because Microsoft makes it so much cheaper than other products. The syntax is a confusing mix of SQL and an object-oriented (OO) dialect of some kind. Compared with full statistical packages, it is weak as well.

Statistical languages such as SAS and SPSS have been around for decades. These products have a large number of options and a great deal of computational power. In the past, you really needed to be an expert to fully use them. Today, they come with a GUI, which makes the coding easier. However, that does not mean you do not need statistical knowledge to make the right decisions.

CHAPTER 7

GROUPING Operators

OLAP FUNCTIONS ADD the ROLLUP and CUBE extensions to the GROUP BY clause. ROLLUP and CUBE are often referred to as supergroups. The grouping operators are used to do the basic reporting we discussed in Chapter 1. They can be written in older standard SQL using GROUP BY and UNION operators.

It is always nice to be able to define a new feature as a shorthand for older operations. The compiler writers can reuse some of the code they already have, and the programmers can reuse some of the mental models they already have. In the case of SQL, it also means that the results of these new features will be SQL tables and not a new kind of data structure, like the classic reports in Chapter 1.

7.1 GROUP BY GROUPING SET

The GROUPING SET (<column list>) is shorthand in SQL-99 for a series of UNIONed queries that are common in reports. For example, to find the total:

```
SELECT dept_name, CAST(NULL AS CHAR(10)) AS job_title,
COUNT(*)
  FROM Personnel
 GROUP BY dept_name
```

```
UNION ALL
SELECT CAST(NULL AS CHAR(8)) AS dept_name, job_title, COUNT(*)
  FROM Personnel
 GROUP BY job_title;
```

This can be rewritten like this:

```
SELECT dept_name, job_title, COUNT(*)
  FROM Personnel
 GROUP BY GROUPING SET (dept_name, job_title);
```

There is a problem with all of the new grouping functions. They will generate NULLs for each dimension at the subtotal levels. How do you tell the difference between a real NULL that was in the data and a generated NULL? This is a job for the GROUPING() function, which returns 0 for NULLs in the original data and 1 for generated NULLs that indicate a subtotal.

Here is a little trick to get a human readable output:

```
SELECT CASE GROUPING(dept_name)
       WHEN 1 THEN 'department total'
       ELSE dept_name END AS dept_name,
       CASE GROUPING(job_title)
       WHEN 1 THEN 'job total'
       ELSE job_title_name END AS job_title
  FROM Personnel
 GROUP BY GROUPING SETS (dept_name, job_title);
```

This is actually a poor programming practice, since the display should be done in the front end and not in the database. Another problem is that you would probably want to use an ORDER BY on the query, rather than get the report back in a random order.

The grouping set concept can be used to define other OLAP groupings.

7.2   ROLLUP

A ROLLUP group is an extension to the GROUP BY clause in SQL-99 that produces a result set that contains subtotal rows in addition to the regular grouped rows. Subtotal rows are super aggregate rows that contain further aggregates, whose values are derived by applying the same column functions that were used to obtain the grouped rows. A ROLLUP grouping is a series of grouping sets as follows:

```
GROUP BY ROLLUP (a, b, c)
```

is equivalent to:

```
GROUP BY GROUPING SETS
(a, b, c)
(a, b)
(a)
()
```

Notice that the (n) elements of the ROLLUP translate to (n + 1) grouping set. Another point to remember is that the order in which the grouping expression is specified is significant for ROLLUP.

The ROLLUP is basically the classic totals and subtotals report presented as a SQL table. The following example is a simple report for three sales regions in 1999. The ROLLUP function is used in the GROUP BY clause.

```
SELECT B.region_nbr, S.city_id, SUM(S.sales) AS total_sales
  FROM SalesFacts AS S, MarketLookup AS M
 WHERE EXTRACT (YEAR FROM trans_date) = 1999
   AND S.city_id = B.city_id
   AND B.region_nbr IN (1, 2, 6)
GROUP BY ROLLUP(B.region_nbr, S.city_id)
ORDER BY B.region_nbr, S.city_id;
```

The SELECT statement behaves in the usual manner. That is, the FROM clause builds a working table, the WHERE clause removes rows that do not meet the search conditions, and the GROUP BY breaks the data into groups that are then reduced to a single row of aggregates and grouping columns. A sample result of the SQL is shown in Table 7.1. The result shows ROLLUP of two groupings (region, city) returning three totals, including region, city, and grand total.

Table 7.1 Yearly Sales by City and Region

```
region_nbr city_id     total_sales
=================================
1              1        81
2              2        13
...            ...      ...
2              NULL     1123  -- region #2
3              11       63
3              12       110
...            ...      ...
3              NULL     1212 — region #3
6              35       55
6              74       13
...            ...      ...
6              NULL     902 — region #6
NULL           NULL     3237 — grand total
```

7.3   CUBES

The CUBE supergroup is the other SQL-99 extension to the GROUP BY clause. It produces a result set that contains all the subtotal rows of a ROLLUP aggregation and, in addition, contains cross-tabulation rows. Cross-tabulation rows are additional superaggregate rows. They are, as the name implies, summaries across columns if the data were represented as a spreadsheet. Like ROLLUP, a CUBE group can also be thought of as a series of grouping sets. In the case of a CUBE, all permutations of the cubed grouping expression are computed along with the grand total. Therefore, the n elements of a CUBE translate to 2n grouping sets.

```
GROUP BY CUBE (a, b, c)
```

is equivalent to:

```
GROUP BY GROUPING SETS
(a, b, c) (a, b) (a, c) (b, c) (a) (b) (c) ()
```

Notice that the three elements of the CUBE translate to eight grouping sets. Unlike ROLLUP, the order of specification of elements doesn't matter for CUBE: CUBE (a, b) is the same as CUBE (b, a). But the rows might not be produced in the same order, depending on your product.

CUBE is an extension of the ROLLUP function. The CUBE function not only provides the column summaries we saw in ROLLUP but also calculates the row summaries and grand totals for the various dimensions. This is a version of crosstabs, as discussed in Chapter 1.

```
SELECT sex_code, race_code, COUNT(*) AS total
  FROM Census
 WHERE EXTRACT (YEAR FROM trans_date) = 1999
 GROUP BY CUBE(sex_code, race_code);
```

Table 7.2 Sex and Race in 1999

```
Sex_code race_code total
=================================
'M'       'Asian'   14
'M'       'White'   12
'M'       'Black'   10
'F'       'Asian'   16
'F'       'White'   11
'F'       'Black'   10
'M'       NULL      36 — column totals
'F'       NULL      37
NULL      'Asian'   30 — row totals
NULL      'White'   23
NULL      'Black'   20
NULL      NULL      73 — grand total
```

7.4   Notes about Usage

If your SQL supports these features, you need to test to see what GROUPING() does with the NULLs created by outer joins. Remember that SQL does not have to return the rows in a table in any particular order. You will still have to put the results into a CURSOR with an ORDER BY clause to produce a report. But you may find that the results tend to come back in sorted order because of the way the SQL engine does its work.

This has happened before. Early versions of SQL did GROUP BY operations with a hidden sort; later SQL products used parallel processing, hashing, and other methods to form the groupings that did not have a sort as a side effect. Always write standard SQL, and do not depend on the internals of one particular release of one particular SQL product.

CHAPTER
8

OLAP Operators in SQL

In CHAPTER 7, WE discussed the new aggregating functions that mimic simple reporting. That is just the beginning. Let me give a bit of history.

IBM and Oracle jointly proposed extensions in early 1999 and, thanks to ANSI's uncommonly rapid actions, they are now part of the SQL-99 standard. IBM implemented portions of the specifications in DB2 UDB 6.2, which was commercially available in some forms as early as mid-1999. Oracle 8i version 2 and DB2 UDB 7.1, both released in late 1999, contain more of these features.

Other vendors contributed, including database tool vendors Brio, MicroStrategy, and Cognos, and database vendor Informix, among others. A team led by Dr. Hamid Pirahesh of IBM's Almaden Research Laboratory played a particularly important role. After his team had researched the subject for about a year and come up with an approach to extending SQL in this area, he called Oracle. The companies then learned that each had independently done some significant work. With Andy Witkowski playing a pivotal role at Oracle, the two companies hammered out a joint standards proposal in about two months. Red Brick was the first product to implement this functionality before the standard but in a less complete form. You can find details in the ANSI document "Introduction to OLAP Functions" by Fred Zemke, Krishna

Kulkarni, Andy Witkowski, and Bob Lyle (*Introduction to OLAP functions*, F. Zemke, K. Kulkarni, A. Witkowski, B. Lyle, ISO/IEC JTC1/SC32 WG3: YGJ-068 = ANSI NCITS H2-99-154r2).

8.1 OLAP Functionality

OLAP functions are a bit different from the GROUP BY family. You specify a "window" defined over the rows over to which an aggregate function is applied and specify the order. When used with a column function, the applicable rows can be further refined, relative to the current row, as either a range or a number of rows preceding and following the current row. For example, within a partition by month, an average can be calculated over the previous three-month period.

8.1.1 Row Numbering

SQL is based on sets that have no ordering, but people depend on ordering to find data. Would you like to have a randomized phone book? In SQL-92 the only ways to add row numbering to a result were to use a cursor (in effect, making the set into a sequential file) or to use a proprietary feature. The vendors' features were all different.

One family uses a pseudocolumn attached to the table. This adds an increasing integer to each row. The IDENTITY column used in SQL Server is the most common example. The first practical consideration is that IDENTITY is proprietary and nonportable, so you know that you will have maintenance problems when you change releases or port your system to other products. Newbies actually think they will never port code! Perhaps they only work for companies that are failing and will be gone. Perhaps their code is so bad nobody else wants their application.

But let's look at the logical problems. First try to create a table with two columns and try to make them both IDENTITY. If you cannot declare more than one column to be of a certain data type, then that thing is not a data type at all, by definition. It is a property, which belongs to the PHYSICAL table rather than the LOGICAL data in the table.

Next, create a table with one column and make it an IDENTITY. Now try to insert, update, and delete different numbers from it. If you cannot insert, update, and delete rows from a table, then it is not a table by definition.

Finally, the ordering used is unpredictable when you insert with a SELECT statement.

```
INSERT INTO Foobar (a, b, c)
SELECT x, y, z
  FROM Floob;
```

Since a query result is a table, and a table is a set that has no ordering, what should the IDENTITY numbers be? The entire, whole, completed set is presented to Foobar all at once, not a row at a time. There are (n!) ways to number (n) rows, so which one do you pick? The traditional answer has been to use whatever the physical order of the result set happened to be. There is that nonrelational phrase "physical order" again!

But it is actually worse than that. If the same query is executed again, but with new statistics or after an index has been dropped or added, the new execution plan could bring the result set back in a different physical order. Indexes and statistics are not part of the logical model.

The second family is to expose the physical location on the disk in an encoded format that can be used to directly move the read/write head to the record. This is the Oracle ROWID. If the disk is defragmented, the location can be changed, and the code will not port. This approach is dependent on hardware.

The third family is a function. This was originally done in Sybase SQL Anywhere (see WATCOM SQL) and was the model for the Standard SQL ROW_NUMBER() function.

This function computes the sequential row number of the row within the window defined by an ordering clause (if one is specified), starting with 1 for the first row and continuing sequentially to the last row in the window. If an ordering clause, ORDER BY, isn't specified in the window, the row numbers are assigned to the rows in arbitrary order as returned by the subselect. In actual code, the numbering functions are used for display purposes rather than adding line numbers in the front end.

A cute trick for the median is to use two ROW_NUMBER()s with an OVER() clause.

```
SELECT AVG(x),
       ROW_NUMBER() OVER(ORDER BY x ASC) AS hi,
       ROW_NUMBER() OVER(ORDER BY x DESC) AS lo
  FROM Foobar
 WHERE hi IN (lo, lo+1, lo-1);
```

This handles both the even and odd number of cases. If there is an odd number of rows, then (hi = lo). If there is an even number of rows, then we want the two values in the two rows to either side of the middle. I leave it to the reader to play with duplicate values in column x and get a weighted median, which is a better measure of central tendency.

```
x   hi  lo
============
1   1   7
1   2   6
2   3   5
3   4   4   <= median — 4.0
3   5   3
3   6   2
3   7   1
```

The median for an even number of cases:

```
x   hi  lo
============
1   1   6
1   2   5
2   3   4 <= median
3   4   3 <= median = 3.5
3   5   2
3   6   1
```

8.1.2   RANK and DENSE_RANK

So far, we have talked about extending the usual SQL aggregate functions. There are special functions that can be used with the window construct.

RANK assigns a sequential rank of a row within a window. The RANK of a row is defined as one plus the number of rows that strictly precede the row. Rows that are not distinct within the ordering of the window are assigned equal ranks. If two or more rows are not distinct with respect to the ordering, then there will be one or more gaps in the sequential rank numbering. That is, the results of RANK may have gaps in the numbers resulting from duplicate values.

```
x   RANK
========
1   1
2   3
2   3
3   5
3   5
3   5
```

```
3    5
3    5
3    5
```

DENSE_RANK also assigns a sequential rank to a row in a window. However, a row's DENSE_RANK is one plus the number of rows preceding it that are distinct with respect to the ordering. Therefore, there will be no gaps in the sequential rank numbering, with ties being assigned the same rank. RANK and DENSE_RANK require an ORDER BY clause.

```
x  DENSE_RANK
==============
1    1
2    2
2    2
3    3
3    3
3    3
3    3
3    3
```

Aside from these functions, the ability to define a window is equally important to the OLAP functionality of SQL. You use windows to define a set of rows over which a function is applied and the sequence in which it occurs. Another way to view the concept of a window is to equate it with the concept of a slice. In other words, a window is simply a slice of the overall data domain.

Moreover, when you use an OLAP function with a column function, such as AVG(), SUM(), MIN(), or MAX(), the target rows can be further refined, relative to the current row, as either a range or a number of rows preceding and following the current row. The point is that you can call upon the entire SQL vocabulary to combine with any of your OLAP-centric SQL statements.

8.1.3   The Window Clause

The window clause has three subclauses: partitioning, ordering, and aggregation grouping. The general format is:

```
<aggregate function> OVER ([PARTITION BY <column list>] ORDER BY
<sort column list> [<aggregation grouping>])
```

A set of column names specifies the partitioning, which is applied to the rows that the preceding FROM, WHERE, GROUP BY, and HAVING clauses produced. If no partitioning is specified, the entire set of rows composes a single partition, and the aggregate function applies to the whole set each time. Though the partitioning looks like a GROUP BY, it is not the same thing. A GROUP BY collapses the rows in a partition into a single row. The partitioning within a window, though, simply organizes the rows into groups without collapsing them.

The ordering within the window clause is like the ORDER BY clause in a CURSOR. It includes a list of sort keys and indicates whether they should be sorted ascending or descending. The important thing to understand is that ordering is applied only within each partition.

The <aggregation grouping> defines a set of rows upon which the aggregate function operates for each row in the partition. Thus, in our example, for each month, you specify the set including it and the two preceding rows. Here is an example from an ANSI paper on the SQL-99 features.

```
SELECT SH.region, SH.month, SH.sales,
       AVG(SH.sales)
       OVER (PARTITION BY SH.region
             ORDER BY SH.month ASC
             ROWS 2 PRECEDING)
       AS moving_average
  FROM SalesHistory AS SH;
```

Here, "AVG(SH.sales) OVER (PARTITION BY...)" is an OLAP function. The construct inside the OVER() clause defines the "window" of data to which the aggregate function, AVG() in this example, is applied.

The window clause defines a partitioned set of rows to which the aggregate function is applied. The window clause says to take the SalesHistory table and then apply the following operations to it:

1.   Partition SalesHistory by region.

2.   Order the data by month within each region.

3.   Group each row with the two preceding rows in the same region.

4.   Compute the moving average on each grouping.

The database engine is not required to perform the steps in the order described here but has to produce the same result set as if they had been carried out.

There are two main types of aggregation groups: physical and logical. In physical grouping, you count a specified number of rows that are before or after the current row. The SalesHistory example used physical grouping. In logical grouping, you include all the data in a certain interval, defined in terms of subset positioned relative to the current sort key. For instance, you create the same group whether you define it as the current month's row plus:

1.   The two preceding rows as defined by the ORDER clause

2.   Any row containing a month no less than two months earlier

Physical grouping works well for contiguous data and programmers who think in terms of sequential files. Physical grouping works for a larger variety of data types than logical grouping, because it does not require operations on values.

Logical grouping works better for data that has gaps or irregularities in the ordering and for programmers who think in SQL predicates. Logical grouping works only if you can do arithmetic on the values (such as numeric quantities and dates).

A physical grouping is based on aggregating a fixed number of rows in a partition, based on their position relative to the row for which the function is computed. One general format is:

```
OVER (RANGE BETWEEN <bound_1> AND <bound_2>)
```

The start of the window, <bound_1>, can be:

```
UNBOUNDED PRECEDING
<unsigned constant> PRECEDING
<unsigned constant> FOLLOWING
CURRENT ROW
```

The meanings are obvious. Unbounded proceeding includes the entire partition that precedes the current row in the sort order. The numbered displacements are done by counting rows.

The end of the window, <bound_2>, can be:

```
UNBOUNDED FOLLOWING
<unsigned constant> PRECEDING
<unsigned constant> FOLLOWING
CURRENT ROW
```

Unbounded following option includes the entire partition that follows the current row in the sort order. For example, you can include the whole partition:

```
OVER (RANGE BETWEEN UNBOUNDED PRECEDING AND UNBOUNDED FOLLOWING)
```

The ROWS option is a shorthand that involves only preceding rows. For example, this is a running accumulative total:

```
SELECT SUM(x)
       OVER (ROWS UNBOUNDED PRECEDING) AS running_total
    FROM Foobar;
```

8.2   NTILE()

NTILE() splits a set into equal groups. It exists in SQL Server and Oracle, but it is not part of the SQL-99 standards. Oracle adds the ability to sort NULLs either FIRST or LAST, but again this is a vendor extension.

```
NTILE(3) OVER (ORDER BY x)
x       NTILE
================
1       1
1       1
2       1
2       1
3       2
3       2
3       2
3       3
3       3
3       3
```

The SQL engine attempts to get the groups the same size, but this is not always possible. The goal is then to have them differ by just one row.

NTILE(n), where (n) is greater than the number of rows in the query, is effectively a ROW_NUMBER(), with groups of size one.

Obviously, if you use NTILE(100), you will get percentiles, but you need at least 100 rows in the result set.

Jeff Moss has been using it for quite some time to work out outliers for statistical analysis of data. An outlier is a value that is outside the range of the other data values. He uses NTILE (200) and drops the first and 200th bucket to rule out the 0.5% on either end of the normal distribution.

If you do not have an NTILE(n) function in your SQL, you can write it with other SQL functions. The SQL Server implementation NTILE(n) function uses a temporary worktable, which can be expensive when the COUNT(*) is not a multiple of (n).

The NTILE(n) puts larger groups before smaller groups in the order specified by the OVER clause. In fact, Marco Russo tested a million row tables, and the following code used 37 times less I/O than the built-in function in SQL Server 2005.

Most of the time, you really don't care about the order of the groups and their sizes; in the real world they will usually vary by one or two rows. You can take the row number, divide it by the bucket size, and find the nearest number plus one.

```
CEILING (ROW_NUMBER()
        OVER (ORDER BY x)
      /((SELECT COUNT(*) + 1.0
           FROM Foobar)/:n))
   AS ntile_bucket_nbr
```

This expression is like this non-OLAP expression:

```
SELECT S1.seq,
      CEILING(((SELECT CAST(COUNT(*)+1 AS FLOAT)
                  FROM Sequence AS S2
                WHERE S2.seq < S1.seq)/:n))
      AS ntile_bucket_nbr
  FROM Sequence AS S1;
```

Do not use this last code segment for a table of more than a few hundred rows. It will run much too long on most products.

8.3   Nesting OLAP functions

One point will confuse older SQL programmers. These OLAP extensions are scalar functions, rather than aggregates. You cannot nest aggregates in standard SQL, because it would make no sense. Consider this example:

```
SELECT customer_id, SUM(SUM(purchase_amt)) --error
  FROM Sales
 GROUP BY customer_id;
```

Each customer should get a total of his or her purchases with the innermost SUM(), which is one number for the grouping. If it worked, the outermost SUM() would be the total of that single number. However, you can write:

```
SUM(SUM(purchase_amt)OVER (PARTITION BY depart_nbr))
```

In this case the total purchase amount for each department is computed and then summed.

8.4   Sample Queries

Probably the most common use of row numbering is for display in the front end. This is not a good thing, since display is supposed to be done in the front end and not in the database. But here it is:

```
SELECT invoice_nbr,
       ROW_NUMBER()
       OVER (ORDER BY invoice_nbr) AS line_nbr,
  FROM Invoices
 ORDER BY invoice_nbr;
```

Now let's try something that is more like a report. List the top five wage earners in the company.

```
SELECT emp_nbr, last_name, sal_tot, sal_rank
  FROM (SELECT emp_nbr, last_name, (salary + bonus)
              RANK()
              OVER (ORDER BY (salary + bonus) DESC)
        FROM Personnel)
```

```
             AS X(emp_nbr, last_name, sal_tot, sal_rank)
      WHERE sal_rank < 6;
```

The derived table X computes the ranking, and then the containing query trims off the top five.

Given a table of sales leads and dealers, we want to match them based on their ZIP codes. Each dealer has a priority, and each lead has a date on which it was received. The dealers with the highest priority get the earlier leads.

```
(SELECT lead_id,
        ROW_NUMBER()
        OVER (PARTITION BY zip_code
                 ORDER BY lead_date)
        AS lead_link
   FROM Leads) AS L
FULL OUTER JOIN
(SELECT dealer_id,
        ROW_NUMBER()
        OVER (PARTITION BY zip_code
                 ORDER BY dealer_priority DESC)
        AS dealer_link
   FROM Dealers) AS D
ON D.dealer_link = L.lead_link
AND D.zip_code = L.zipcode;
```

You can add more criteria to the ORDER BY list or create a lookup table with multiparameter scoring criteria.

These new features give the SQL programmer the ability to do simple reporting within SQL. I have mixed feelings about this, but they mean that we will have a single portable syntax instead of many proprietary report writer syntaxes.

CHAPTER

9

Sparseness in Cubes

THE CONCEPT OF cubes is a nice way to get a graphic image when you are thinking about reporting data. Think about a simple spreadsheet with columns that hold the dates of a shipment and rows that hold the particular product shipped on that date. Obviously, this is going to be a large spreadsheet if the company has, say, 10,000 items and five years of history to look at (3,652,500 cells, actually).

Most of these cells will be empty. But there is a subtle difference between empty, zero, and NULL. Empty is a spreadsheet term, and it means the cell exists because it was created by the range of rows and columns when the spreadsheet was set up. Zero is a numeric value; it needs to be in a cell to exist, and you cannot divide by it—it is really a number. NULLs are a SQL concept that hold a place for a missing or unknown value. Remember that NULLs propagate in simple computations, and they do require storage in SQL—they are not the same as an empty cell.

Imagine that we did not ship iPods before October 23, 2001, because they were not released before that date. This cell does not exist in the cube yet. And in October of 2001, we had an inventory of red velvet hip-hugger bell bottoms; we sold none of them (the same as every month since 1976); this is a zero. Finally, nobody has reported iPod shipments for 2006-03-25 yet, but we know it is a hot item and we will have made sales. Now we add a column for iPods, and a history of empty cells appears.

At this point, you need to decide how to handle these cases. I would recommend ignoring nonexistent iPods in any sales history reports. Your cube tool should be able to tell the difference between all three cases. But the long history of not selling red velvet hip-hugger bell bottoms (i.e., shipments = 0) is important information—hey, disco is dead and you need to clean out the inventory.

A NULL is also information, but, more properly, it is a sign that data is missing. This is trickier, because you need to have methods for handling that missing data.

Can you estimate a value and use it? If my iPod sales have increased at a steady rate of p-% per month for the last (m) months, can I assume the trend will continue? Or should I use a median or an average? Or should I use data up to the point that I know values?

9.1   Hypercube

Extend the spreadsheet model from two dimensions to three, four, five, and so forth. Human beings have serious problems with a graphic greater three dimensions. The universe in which we live and see things is limited to three dimensions.

Enough cells will be empty that it is vital that the storage for the cube has a sparse matrix implementation. That means we do not physically store empty cells, but they might be materialized inside the engine. Figure 9.1 is a diagram for a (sources, routes, time) cube. I will explain the hierarchies on the three axes.

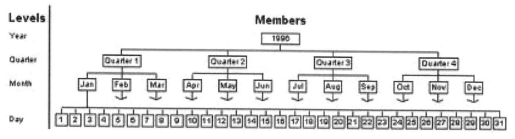

Figure 9.1 Dimension Hierarchy as a Tree

9.2   Dimensional Hierarchies

A listing of all of the cells in a hypercube is useless. We want to see aggregated (summary) information. We want to know that iPod sales are increasing, that we need to get rid of those bell bottoms, that most of our business is in North America, and so forth.

Aggregation means that we need a hierarchy on the dimensions. Here is an example of a temporal dimension. Writing a hierarchy in SQL is easily done with a nested sets model if you have to write your own code.

```
CREATE TABLE TemporalDim
(range_name CHAR(15) NOT NULL PRIMARY KEY,
range_start_date DATE NOT NULL,
range_end_date DATE NOT NULL,
 CHECK (range_start_date < range_end_date));

INSERT INTO TemporalDim
VALUES ('Year2006', '2006-01-01', '2006-12-31'),
     ('Qtr-01-2006', '2006-01-01', '2006-03-31'),
     ('Mon-01-2006', '2006-01-01', '2006-01-31'),
     ('Day:2006-01-01', '2006-01-01', '2006-01-01'),
      ..;
```

You can argue that you do not need to go to the leaf node level in the hierarchy, but only to the lowest level of aggregation. That will save space, but the code can be trickier when you have to show the leaf node level of the hierarchy. (See Figure 9.2.)

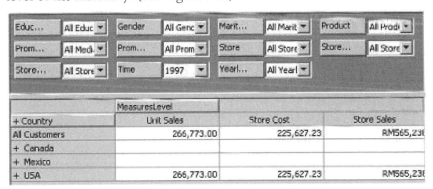

Figure 9.2 Typical OLAP Interface

This is the template for a hierarchical aggregation.

```
SELECT TD.range_name, ..
  FROM TemporalDim AS TD, FactTable AS F
 WHERE F.shipping_time BETWEEN TD.range_start_date
                AND range_end_date;
```

If you do not have the leaf nodes in the temporal dimension, then you need to add a CTE with the days and their names that are at the leaf nodes in your query.

```
WITH Calendar (date_name, cal_date)
AS VALUES (CAST ("2006-01-01" AS CHAR(15)),
           CAST ('2006-01-01' AS DATE),
           ("2006-01-02",'2006-01-02'),
           etc.
SELECT TD.range_name, ..
  FROM TemporalDim AS TD, FactTable AS F
 WHERE F.shipping_time BETWEEN TD.range_start_date
                 AND range_end_date
UNION ALL
SELECT Calendar.date_name, ..
  FROM Calendar AS C, FactTable AS F
 WHERE C.cal_date = F.shipping_time;
```

Note the use of double quote marks around the ISO-8601 format calendar date name. The calendar table is used for other queries in the OLTP side of the house, so you should already have it in at least one database. You may also find that your cube tool automatically returns data at the leaf level if you ask it.

9.3   Drilling and Slicing

Many of the OLAP user interface tools will have a display with a drop-down menu for each dimension, which lets you pick the level of aggregation in the report. The analogy is the slide switches on the front of expensive stereo equipment, which set how the music will be played, but not which songs are on the CD. It is called drill down, because you start at the highest level of the hierarchies and travel down the tree structure. Figure 9.3 is an example of such an interface from a Microsoft reporting tool.

Slicing a cube is another physical analogy. Look at the illustration of the cube, and imagine that you have a cheese knife and you slice off blocks from the cube. For example, we might want to look at only the ground shipments, so we slice off just that dimension, building a subcube. The drill downs will still be in place. This is like picking the song from a CD.

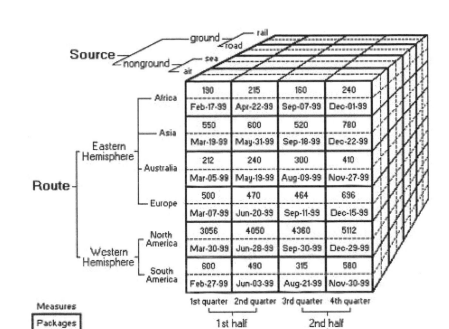

Figure 9.3 Example Interface

(*Source*: http://www.aspfree.com/c/a/MS-SQL-Server/Accessing-OLAP-using-ASP-dot-NET/)

CHAPTER 10

Data Quality

DATA STINKS. The trade press is full of articles that quote very depressing error rates in credit reports, medical records, and corporate data. You can get white papers from sources such as the Data Warehousing Institute and PriceWaterhouse (now part of IBM) that put the cost to businesses of poor-quality data in the billions of dollars.

There is even a federal law (Public Law 106-554; H.R. 5658, Section 515) that directs the Office of Management and Budget to issue governmentwide guidelines that "provide policy and procedural guidance to federal agencies for ensuring and maximizing the quality, objectivity, utility, and integrity of information (including statistical information) disseminated by federal agencies.(Public Law 106-554; H.R. 5658. Sectioon 515)" Agencies had to issue their own implementation guidelines by October 1, 2002.

Typical ways that an organization finds out that its data is bad include the following:

1. The organization is named in a lawsuit. There is approximately one lawyer for every 400 people in the United States, and they love civil actions. The result is a quick attempt to mop up the spill, but all too often there is no attempt to fix the leak.

2.   The organization wants to conform to a law, such as Sarbanes-Oxley, which requires audit trails. But the audit trails have dead ends, such as missing invoice numbers that come from using autoincremented features in a particular SQL product that leaves gaps, keeping the same data element in different data types, and so forth.

3.   The organization does a data warehouse project, and data from multiple sources is gathered in raw form in one place for the first time. There are some great horror stories about the discovery of bad data, and I will get to a few of them later.

4.   The organization is proactive and begins an actual data quality program.

The fourth case is rare, but it does occur. The fact that we now have software tools for checking data quality helps quite a bit, but you can do some simple tests with a few basic SQL queries.

10.1 Checking Columns for Value Counts

One question is: How many distinct values does each column of a table have? One way to find out in some products is to query the schema statistics table, if the product keeps that information. But if you are not that lucky, you can always get out the table and corresponding column names, and then use a text editor to generate queries with this template. Assume we have a table that looks like this:

```
CREATE TABLE Foobar
(known_key CHAR(2) NOT NULL PRIMARY KEY,
 actual_key CHAR(2) NOT NULL,
 non_key CHAR(2) NOT NULL,
 non_key_null CHAR(2));
INSERT INTO Foobar VALUES
 ('K1', 'a', 'x', 'a'), ('K2', 'b', 'x', NULL),
 ('K3', 'c', 'x', 'b'), ('K4', 'd', 'y', 'c'),
 ('K5', 'e', 'y', 'd'), ('K6', 'f', 'y', 'e');
```

Use a text editor to generate a query like this:

```
SELECT 'Foobar' AS table_name,
       COUNT(DISTINCT known_key) AS known_key,
```

```
      COUNT(DISTINCT actual_key) AS actual_key,
      COUNT(DISTINCT non_key) AS non_key,
      COUNT(DISTINCTnon_key_null) AS non_key_null
FROM Foobar;
```

You can also modify this basic query to find other characteristics of the columns of a table, such as whether a column is a candidate key (i.e., NOT NULL UNIQUE) without using the schema information tables. The COUNT(DISTINCT <col name>) templates are replaced by :

```
CASE WHEN COUNT(DISTINCT <col_name>) = COUNT(*)
     THEN 'Y' ELSE 'N' END AS "<col_name>"
```

These should run faster than a cursor placed over each column. However, you can also obtain data profiling tools (Evoke AXIO is one example) to do this task.

The schema information tables in many products will also have statistics that you can read. They are used by the optimizer to speed up queries, rather than to check the data quality, so they tend to describe the statistical distribution of the nonkey data elements in a histogram, have the extrema for numeric and temporal data, and perhaps contain some frequency information.

10.2 Finding Rules in a Schema

When you are checking to see if a database is "following the rule," you can first pull out the CHECK() constraint logic and be fairly certain that those rules are enforced. If a CHECK() constraint was added to the schema after bad data was inserted, you need to know whether your database product will automatically run a check on the existing data or whether the constraint goes into effect only for future changes. This sounds crazy, but there are products that have had this design flaw.

Do not confuse this with deferred constraint checking. That is a feature in SQL-92 that allows the database to be in an illegal state during a session. But all constraints must be met by the end of that session. Here is the full syntax:

```
[CONSTRAINT <constraint name>]
  { NOT NULL | UNIQUE | PRIMARY KEY | DEFAULT value | CHECK (
<search condition>) |
    REFERENCES <table name> [(<column>)]
```

```
[MATCH FULL | MATCH PARTIAL]
[ON DELETE <action>]
[ON UPDATE <action>]
[DEFERRABLE | NOT DEFERRABLE]
[INITIALLY DEFERRED | INITIALLY IMMEDIATE]}
```

The DEFERRABLE option says that you can turn off the constraint; NOT DEFERRABLE is self-explanatory. The INITIALLY DEFERRED option says that this is the state of the constraint until you change it in the session or the session ends. The INITIALLY IMMEDIATE option is opposite; the constraint is applied at each statement in the session until you turn it off.

Full and partial matching is another topic, and it is not yet widely implemented.

Another thing to remember is that the logical rules for DML and DDL are different in SQL. The WHERE and ON clauses in DML will select rows for which the search condition tests TRUE. The CHECK() constraint will allow rows for which the search condition tests TRUE or UNKNOWN. The reason for this was to allow NULLs in the NULL-able columns. But you will find that many NULL-able columns should not be NULL-able in a poorly designed schema and that a lot of dirty data has accumulated.

To make things worse, a UNIQUE constraint allows one NULL, but if your product allows NULLs in unique indexes, it may allow multiple NULLs in a column. This means that we have two different definitions of uniqueness.

It is important to distinguish between data errors and exceptional cases. For example, if a customer is assigned to a particular salesperson, and we find a few transactions that were posted to different salespeople, we will suspect an error. But the reason might be that the regular salesperson was on jury duty or out sick, and the customer was assigned a temporary salesperson.

I cannot enforce the salesperson-customer assignment with simple declarative referential integrity, because it is not a 100% of the time rule. One approach is a percentage-based approach to the exceptions. In this case, we might set the bar at a "98% of the time, a customer has one and only one assigned salesperson" rule and pull the exceptions to it. Another way would be to set a fixed number of exceptions: a rule stating that "a customer has one and only one assigned salesperson, with up to five exceptions."

This can be done with the CREATE ASSERTION statement in standard SQL-92. This is a CHECK() constraint that is not attached to any table or column, but to the schema as a whole.

```
CREATE ASSERTION ExceptionCounts
AS
CHECK (5 <= ALL (SELECT COUNT(DISTINCT salesman_id)
                 FROM SalesHistory
  GROUP BY customer_acct));
```

The same constraint can appear in a table CHECK() clause. But all constraints are assumed to be true for an empty table, including attempts to check to see that the table is not empty.

But what if we really don't know what our rules are? What about the rules that are a result of the way we do business, rather than the rules we set up? Perhaps 80% of the time, a customer places an order with the same salesperson. Not because of company policy, but because our stores are widely spread apart, so customers tend to go to the same branch at the same time of day. That is how you get to be a "regular" at your local coffee shop and know the waitress that serves you at your favorite table.

This rule is not in the constraints, but in the data. It is just as good a predictor and scrubbing tool as a policy rule. You want to go through the database and measure the likelihood of a change in such patterns. Why hasn't Mary Jones built up some regular customers? Perhaps she is a floater who works at many of our locations, perhaps she is too new to have regulars, or perhaps she pours hot coffee on people so nobody does business with her more than once.

What sort of rules do I want to specify at this level? There are basically three types: mathematical relationships, logical rules (if-then or Horn clauses), and pattern rules (spelling, regular expressions). This is a simple breakdown of the types of rules; you will see other categorizations in the industry that are more complex.

10.2.1 Mathematical Rules

An example of a mathematical rule might be:

```
Volume = height * 3.14159 * radius ^ 2.0
```

I might want to look at exceptions that occur outside of 99% of the rows, because it would mean I am getting a weird rounding error in my floating-point computation.

As an example of a product for this type of investigation, WizRule (http://www.hallogram.com) looks for all the arithmetic formulas with up to five variables that hold in the database. You can also use a statistical tool, such as SAS or SPSS, or other math software tools.

What if I do not know the relationship among my data elements? The tools can fit the data to equations. You can then use these equations as part of a quality checking process, but you have to have faith that the data that was used to get these equations was clean.

At one extreme, we can look for a simple linear formula ($Y = a * X + b$) with a few arguments. At the other extreme, the software can discover a complicated polynomial or an exponential formula in the data. But you can fit *any* data to a complicated polynomial. Such a formula might not have any real meaning and be so complicated that it is of little use.

There is also the "fear factor"—nonmathematical users do not feel comfortable with exponential or long mathematical expressions. The number of arguments in the formula should be fewer than six.

We will discuss some of the more common distributions that a single column can have later.

10.2.2 Logical Rules

An example of a logical rule might be expressed as:

```
IF customer_name  = 'Hilary Duff'
   AND branch_nbr = 12
THEN salesperson_name = 'Joe Celko':
```

I want to set the probability of success (say, 95% of time), and I want to know the size of the population (larger is better).

At the extreme end of logical rules are decision tables, such as Logic Gem (http://www.catalyst.com/products/logicgem). Think of a decision table as a spreadsheet for logic. They are used to generate programs, but we can use them to check data quality.

The screen is divided into four main areas; one holds each condition on a line in a vertical list. The rules are in columns next to the condition. Each cell in the rule can have a "y," "n," or "–" in it: "y" is short for "Yes" and means the condition is true in this rule; "n" means "No" and the condition is false; "–" means "do not care" because the condition does not matter for this rule.

On the lower part of the screen, you will see a list of actions under the conditions. The vertical rule columns continue down the screen. The user can specify the action to be taken when a rule applies. The actions are usually code in some programming language.

As a very simple example, assume that when we assign an employee a company car, he or she can get a company gasoline credit card or buy his or her own gas and get reimbursed. If you have a company credit card, then you must have a company car—they are not for private use.

Assigned a company car	Y	Y	N	N	N
Reimbursed for gasoline	Y	N	N	–	–
Uses company gas card	N	N	N	Y	–
ACCEPT	X		X		X
REJECT		X		X	

The actions can be as simple as "accept" or "reject" for data quality purposes. But you can also assign a score with the actions. This is a first attempt at filling out the eight possible cases in this problem. When the rules are in the decision table, you can automatically check for the following:

1. Ambiguous rules

2. Contradictory rules

3. Missing rules

4. Redundant rules

This example is missing a rule for the employee who buys his or her own gas for a company car. The two rules on the right contradict each other, and we need to remove one of them. I can now go back and change the grid until I get a valid rule for all possible situations. This is not impressive for only three conditions, but H & R Block used Logic Gem to investigate the U.S. tax code for logical problems.

10.2.3 Pattern Rules

A pattern rule might involve something as simple as matching a code from a known set of values. For example, one table might use "M" and "F" for a sex code, so we know that any character not on that list is bad data.

Checking spelling is harder, since it is not always possible to create a complete list, so we have to resort to statistics. If a very common spelling differs from a much less common spelling, then the less common spelling might be in error. The most common errors are (a) a missing single letter, (b) an extra letter, (c) a wrong letter, and (d) a pairwise transpose. This lets us write a routine to come up with all the permutations of the letters in a suspected word.

Another pattern rule can be based on regular expressions. These are good for checking industry standard codes and internal encodings. You can find tools and tutorials at http://www.regular-expressions.info. A regular expression is a pattern that is used to match character strings. You can find lots of resources for details on regular expressions. For example, an email address has this regular expression pattern:

```
\b[A-Z0-9._%-]+@[A-Z0-9.-]+\.[A-Z]{2,4}\b
```

The version used in standard SQL's SIMILAR TO predicate is based on the POSIX version of grep(). There are many versions and extensions; however, if your SQL does not support it, you can find a package and use it in a host program or embed it into a CREATE PROCEDURE using another programming language. If you do have such a predicate, you should have a CHECK() constraint on all your character string columns that already hold encodings. The data can still be wrong, but at least it will be formatted correctly.

Some errors cannot be detected by rule construction. A person seeing a list of customers named "Mickey Mouse," "Would Not Tell," "Rt1%$&5768," and "clive@ibm.com" would be aware that the first name is a fraud, the second is a comment (not a relative of "William Tell"), the third is garbage, and the fourth is an email address that might be used to get the name.

SSA and Melissa Data are companies that sell software for scrubbing names. It is complicated enough that you really do need specialized software.

10.3 Feedback for Data Quality

Graeme Simsion has a wonderful phrase in his lectures on data quality and management: "Mop the floor, but then fix the leak!" which means that it is not enough to fix a data problem now—you need to investigate and find a way to prevent it in the future.

One simple example is the discovery during the creation of a data warehouse that some systems use CHAR(8) and others use CHAR(9) for a part number. The company clearly needs to set up one definition in the data dictionary and then standardize the entire enterprise on that definition.

A more complicated example was given by Mike Jones ("Improving on the Doctor's Orders," *Baseline*, March 2006, p. 28). He works for a children's hospital that installed a computerized order system to replace a manual system. The first effect was a 75% reduction in medication errors and a 33% reduction in errors related to lab tests. Yes, it is true that doctors cannot read their own handwriting.

However, there was a 33% increase in "undesirable pharmacy interventions." This is a medical term that means the pharmacy had to call the doctor to get clarifications about an order. In the manual system, the child's weight was estimated by each doctor and a dosage computed in his or her head. In the computerized system, the patient's weight was known before the dosage was computed. If two doctors entered different weights, the system will flag it. The pharmacist would then call the doctor and get a correction. Since the pharmacist has no idea what the patient looks like and only manual records to go by, a typographical error could have turned a 90 lb. kid into a 9-lb. infant or vice versa. I would say that phone call is a highly desirable intervention!

10.4 Further Reading

There are lots of resources for regular expressions. Here is a quick list:

Mastering Regular Expressions, Second Edition, by Jeffrey Friedl; ISBN 0-59600289-0, O'Reilly, July 2002.

Sams Teach Yourself Regular Expressions in 10 Minutes, by Ben Forta; ISBN 0672325667; Sams, 1997-2006.

Regular Expression Pocket Reference by Tony Stubblebine; ISBN 059600415X; O'Reilly, 2003.

Regular Expression Recipes: A Problem-Solution Approach, by Nathan A. Good; ISBN: 1590594975, Apress, 2005.

Beginning Regular Expressions (Programmer to Programmer), by Andrew Watt; ISBN 0764574892, Wrox Press, 2005,

In particular, if you use Oracle, you might want look at this book.

Oracle Regular Expressions Pocket Reference by Jonathan Gennick and Peter Linsley (*Programmer to Programmer*); ISBN 0596006012, Wrox Press, 2005,

Beginning Regular Expressions (Programmer to Programmer), by Andrew Watt

CHAPTER 11

Correlation

CORRELATIONS IN BUSINESS analytics are an attempt predict the future and discover "laws of nature" in existing data. The classic folklore story is that a chain of convenience stores found that men in their twenties who purchase beer on Fridays after work are also likely to buy a pack of diapers. So, if you put the Pampers next to the Budweiser, sales of both would increase.

As many versions of this story circulated, people would propose causes for the relationship. The most common version was that "Joe Six-Pack" gets paid on Fridays, wants his beer, and has to get the diapers to keep the wife happy. I had the theory that "Jane Six-Pack" gets Joe's check and has to get the diapers herself. She has been with the kids all week and wants the beer more than Joe does.

Correlations are probably the "easiest ones of the hard stuff" to understand, so, of course, they are the most often misrepresented and misunderstood. First of all, correlation is not cause and effect. Causes determine effects, like the laws of physics and math. A correlation is a number that expresses a relationship between two measurements, which can change over time, or be the result of purely random events.

A "necessary cause" is something that must be present for an effect to happen—a car must have gas to run. A "sufficient cause" will bring about the effect by itself—dropping a hammer on your foot will make you scream in pain, but so will having your hard drive crash. A "contributory cause" is one that helps the effect along but would not be necessary or sufficient by itself to create the effect. Loading Windows 95 on your home computer will not cause a crash per se, but it will contribute to it.

There are also coincidences, where one thing happens at the same time as another, but without a causal relationship at all.

A correlation between two measurements, say X and Y, is basically a formula that lets you predict one measurement, given the other, plus or minus some error range. For example, if I shot a cannon locked at a certain angle and with a certain amount of gunpowder, I could expect to place the cannonball within a relatively small radius of the target most of the time. Once in a while, the cannonball will be dead on target, and other times it could land several meters away, thanks to variation in the shape and weight of the cannonball, the quality of the powder, the wind, and a million other immeasurable things. But my formula is good enough to wage a war.

The strength of the prediction is called the coefficient of correlation and is denoted by the variable r, where $(-1 < = r < = 1)$ in statistics. A coefficient of correlation of -1 is absolute negative correlation—when X happens, then Y never happens. Absolute positive correlation is $+1$—when X happens, then Y always happens. A zero coefficient of correlation means that X and Y happen independently of each other.

A correlation of 0.7 or better is gratifying in the real world, but medical science wants a 95% or better confidence level. Their errors kill people. This is why the tables in the back of statistics books have columns for 90%, 95%, and 98% confidence levels.

The confidence level is related to the coefficient of the correlation, but it is expressed as a percentage. It says that x% of the time, the relationship you have will not happen by chance.

The March 1994 issue of *Discover* magazine included commentary columns entitled "Counting on Dyscalculia" by John Allen Paulos, the man who coined the word "innumeracy" in his 1990 bestseller of the same title. His particular topic was health statistics, because those create a lot of "pop dread" when they get played in the media.

One of his examples in the article was a widely covered lawsuit by a man who alleged a causal connection between his wife's frequent use of a cellular phone and her subsequent brain cancer. But brain cancer is a rare disease that strikes approximately 7 out of 100,000 people per year. Given the large population of the United States, this is still about 17,500 new cases per year, and that number has held pretty steady for years.

There were an estimated 10 million cellular phone users in the United States in the mid 1990s, and I have no idea what the current figure is. If there were a causal relationship, then there would be an increase in brain cancer cases as cellular phone usage increased. In fact, if we found that there were fewer than 7,000 cases among cellular phone users, we could use the same "argument" to "prove" that cellular phones prevent brain cancer.

And sure enough, over the years, the majority of studies show no link between cell phones and cancer.

11.1 Causes and Correlation

There are five ways two variables can be related to each other. The truth could be that X causes Y. You can estimate the chirp rate of a cricket from the temperature in Fahrenheit using the formula (chirps = 3.777 ∞ degree F – 137.22), with r = 0.9919 accuracy. However, nobody believes that crickets cause temperature changes.

The second case is that Y causes X. Remember that a correlation does not point in one direction only. You can do a little algebra and write the same formula in terms of X or Y.

The third case is that X and Y interact with each other. Supply and demand curves in classic economics are an example where as one goes up, the other goes down (negative feedback in computer terms). A more horrible example is drug addiction, where the user requires larger and larger doses to get the desired effect (positive feedback in computer terms), as opposed to a habituation, where the usage hits an upper level and stays there.

The fourth case is that any relationship is pure chance. Any two trends in the same direction will have some correlation, so it should not surprise you that once in a while, two will match very closely.

The final case is where the two variables are effects of other variable(s), which are outside the study. The most common unseen variables are changes in a common environment. For example, severe hay fever attacks go up when corn prices go down. They share a common element—good weather. Good weather means a bigger corn crop and hence lower prices, but it also means more ragweed and pollen and hence more hay fever attacks.

Since the formula for calculating the correlation coefficient standardizes the variables, changes in scale or units of measurement will not affect its value. For this reason, the correlation coefficient is often more useful than a graphical depiction in determining the strength of the association between two variables.

11.2 Linear Correlation

We like fitting data to linear formulas. They are simple and easy to use. Linear formulas sum a set of values multiplied by a weight, which can be positive or negative to get an answer. The formulas look like this:

```
Value to be predicted = (weight_1 * value_1)
+ (weight_2 * value_2)
+..
+ (weight_n * value_n)
+ error
```

If we were dealing with pure mathematics, the error would be zero; if we were dealing with physics, the errors would be small. But we are dealing with databases, so the errors will be within a wider range.

However, there are some serious problems with the technique.

11.2.1 Pearson's r

The correlation coefficient always takes a value between −1 and 1, with 1 or −1 indicating perfect correlation (all points would lay along a straight line in this case). A positive correlation indicates a positive association between the variables (increasing values in one variable corresponds to increasing values in the other variable), while a negative correlation indicates a negative association between the variables (increasing values in one variable corresponding to decreasing values in the other variable). A correlation value close to 0 indicates no association between the variables.

Since the formula for calculating the correlation coefficient standardizes the variables, changes in scale or units of measurement will not affect its value. For this reason, the correlation coefficient is often more useful than a graphical depiction in determining the strength of the association between two variables.

The usual test is "Pearson's r" or the correlation coefficient, which in effect draws a straight line through the data and gives us a measure of how far the real data is from the predictive model. You obviously want to pick the formula with the best fit.

If the relationship is not a simple linear one, this is not going to find it. There are many other possible relationships. For example, a fad may have an exponential growth, which that then decays sharply, rather than linear growth.

What should you do with NULLs in a computation of Pearson's r?

There are several options: If (x, y) = (NULL, NULL), then my query will drop them both and the answer stays the same. That seems to follow the usual SQL aggregate function rules for singleton stats such as AVG() about dropping NULLs before computing. That was the reason for using COUNT(x) and not COUNT(*) in the code to be shown shortly.

But what is the correct (or reasonable) behavior if (x, y) has one and only one NULL in the pair? My initial thoughts are:

1. Drop the pair. That is quick and easy with a "WHERE x IS NOT NULL AND y IS NOT NULL" clause.

2. Convert (x, NULL) to (x, AVG(x)) and (NULL, y) to (AVG(y), y) or some expression that will smooth out the missing values.

3. Should the code use COUNT(*) instead of COUNT(x) to show that the missing values are affecting the answer?

Here is a set of observations (x1, y1), (x2, y2), ... (xn, yn). The formula for computing the correlation coefficient is given by this query:

```
CREATE TABLE RawData
(x REAL NOT NULL,
 y REAL NOT NULL);
```

Sample data with r = 0.9608:

```
INSERT INTO RawData
VALUES (1.0, 2.0), (2.0, 5.0), (3.0, 6.0);

SELECT (SUM(x*y) - ((SUM(x)*SUM(y))/COUNT(x)))
       /(SQRT((SUM(x*x)- (SUM(x)*SUM(x)/COUNT(x)))
        *(SUM(y*y)-(SUM(y)*SUM(y)/COUNT(x))))))
       AS pearson_r
FROM RawData;
-- person_r = 0.9608
```

SQRT() is part of SQL-99, but all products have square root and power functions for years.

```
WITH A(ax, ay) AS (SELECT AVG(x), AVG(y) FROM RawData)
SELECT SUM((x - A.ax) * (y - A.ay))
       / SQRT (SUM (POWER (x - A.ax, 2.0)) + SUM (POWER (y - A.ay,
2.0)))
 FROM RawData;
```

Matthias Klaey ran a quick test for all of these options in Ingres, Linux Version II 3.0.1 (int.lnx/109).

Replace the NULLs with –99 as a dummy value:

```
SELECT COALESCE(x, -99), COALESCE(y, -99)
FROM Foobar ;
```

```
Foobar
x                y
===================
   3.000   -99.000
   5.000   -99.000
   7.000   -99.000
 -99.000     1.000
 -99.000     2.000
 -99.000     3.000
 -99.000     4.000
   3.000     6.000
   5.000    11.000
   7.000    14.000
   1.000     2.000
```

```
SELECT CORR(x, y) FROM Foobar;
```

This returns 0.000.

```
SELECT CORR(x, y) FROM Foobar
 WHERE x IS NOT NULL
   AND y IS NOT NULL;
```

This returns 1.000.

```
INSERT INTO Foobar (x, y) VALUES (3.0, 2.0)
SELECT CORR(x, y) FROM Foobar
 WHERE x IS NOT NULL
   AND y IS NOT NULL;
```

This returns 0.94.

The good news is that r is immune to linear transformations on the inputs. The bad news is that this is a numerically unstable algorithm. The addition of a few outliers to the data can make a radical change in r. I have given a bibliography at the end of this chapter if you want to see the math. The practical solution is usually to remove outliers or to do resampling.

11.2.2   The Rashomon Effect

Have you ever seen the classic Japanese movie *Rashomon* (1950, directed by Akira Kurosawa, starring Akira Kurosawa)? The film tells the story of a rape and murder by a bandit, as seen in flashbacks from four different viewpoints. The stories are all different but lead to the same outcome.

Given a set of 30 variables, you can pick a subset of 5 variables from which to get a correlation. The problem is that you have 142,506 possible subsets. How do you pick the right attributes for your correlation?

We have two problems. One is the sheer number of subsets we already mentioned. The second problem is that many of these subsets will have an acceptable value, yet be completely different attributes. At this point, you need human judgment to pick a subset of attributes. People can avoid silly combinations (shoe size, annual chocolate consumption, and house number), but people tend to favor things that are familiar and easy to obtain.

11.3   Nesting Functions

Correlation looks for a formula of the form $y = A * x + B$, where A is the slope of the line and B is the y-intercept. However, growth patterns are often exponential, not linear, so they follow $y = A * (EXP(x)) + B$ patterns.

One of the nice things about having a CORR(x, y) function in your SQL is that you can make one or both of the parameters expressions. In particular, you can use LN(), EXP(), and POWER() functions to see growth patterns.

But what curves should we be looking at and why? That is the next topic.

11.4 Further Reading

For the details on the "beer and diapers" myth, see the following:
    http://web.onetel.net.uk/~hibou/Beer%20and%20Nappies.html
    http://www.praxagora.com/andyo/ar/privacy_mines.html

For the "cancer and cell phones" correlation, see the following:
    http://jncicancerspectrum.oxfordjournals.org/cgi/content/full/
    jnci;93/3/170

For the painful details, see the following:
    Tony F. Chan, Gene H. Golub, and Randall J. LeVeque, "Algorithms for Computing the Sample Variance: Analysis and Recommendations," *The American Statistician*, August. 1983, Vol. 37, No. 3, pp. 242–247.

    The earliest reference in this chapter goes back to B. P. Welford, "Note on a Method for Calculating Corrected Sums of Squares and Products," *Technometrics*, 1962, Vol. 4, pp. 419–420.

Also look at:
    http://www.amstat.org/publications/tas/
    http://www.amstat.org/publications/technometrics/

CHAPTER
12

Data Distributions

DATA IN THE aggregate falls into patterns, which are called distribution curves in statistics. We like patterns to come out of data. They give us predictability, trends, and knowledge at a higher level.

Distributions are based on how many times each value appears in a given set. The shapes of these distributions are often approximated by formulas on continuous variables.

These distributions are not arbitrary; rather, there are actual physical reasons that they appear in data. But they are not exact in real data.

12.1 Flat Distribution

This is the easiest one; all the values are unique, so you get a straight line if you graph it. This distribution occurs when you are looking at identifiers. It almost sounds silly to include it as a distribution at all, but it is important when it is violated in a table. You do not want to have two products with the same inventory control number and so forth.

But the unique identifiers get used in other tables to assure that their distributions are valid. For example, at the start of a product category's life cycle, it will show a Zipfian distribution because ther will be a few very popular brands that sell well. Later competition, staturation and replacement products will bend the sales into a Logisitics curve or a short supply will create a Poisson curve. Let's talk about those other distributions.

12.2 Zipfian Distribution

The Zipfian distribution is named after the Harvard linguistic professor George Kingsley Zipf (1902–1950). A Zipfian distribution occurs when some values appear much more often than others. When you diagram it on a graph with logarithm scales on both axes, you get a straight line (see Figure 12.1). It was originally discovered in linguistics by Herman Zipf, who observed that the more common a word is in a written language, the shorter it tends to be. But the same thing happens in other areas—you sell more cheap goods than expensive, and so forth.

A common example would be book sales. A new Best Seller will sell millions of copies in a short time, then sales drop rapidly as it is replaced by the next Best Seller. In the old days, a book would go out of print as its sales slid down the tail of a Zipfian curve to the point that the book is not worth keeping in print. Today, however, the cost of reprinting is much lower than in the days of metal type. This has led to what is called "The Long Tail" in Internet marketing (http://www.wired.com/wired/archive/12.10/tail.html); look at the shape of Zipfian curve and you can see where the name comes from.

The particulars will vary over time, because a slight change in a worst-sellers volume becomes a huge change. I was the best-selling author on Amazon.com in the United Kingdom for a few days because someone bought a case of my books for a class. I was quickly knocked back down the list when nobody bought a case of books the next week and someone named Tom Clancy released a spy novel.

Zipf curves follow a straight line when plotted on a double-logarithmic grid, as shown in Figure 12.1.

This distribution was first developed for linguistics, so it is not surprising that Web page usage seems to follow a Zipfian distribution. The home page gets a lot of hits, and then other pages trail off.

Your choice of graphical presentation depends on your audience. Linear scales are easier to understand for most people. But it is easier to draw some distributions on log-log and semi-log paper, which can be handy for research.

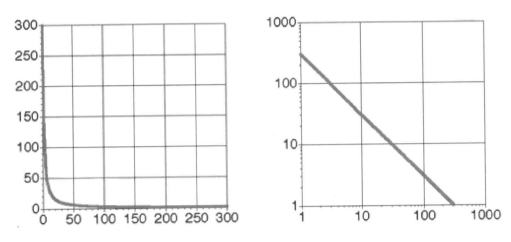

Linear scales on both axes   *Logarithmic scales on both axes*

Figure 12.1 Plots of a Zipf distribution with 300 rows.

12.3 Gaussian, Normal, or Bell Curve

This distribution, called a Gaussian or normal distribution or a bell curve, occurs when you average the averages of random samples from any distribution. This is the effect you get when you have a lot of independent or near-independent factors contributing to a value. It is referred to as a normal distribution because that is how the real world works.

The classic example is grades on a school exam. Each question on an exam is independent of the others and the answers have different averages for right answers.

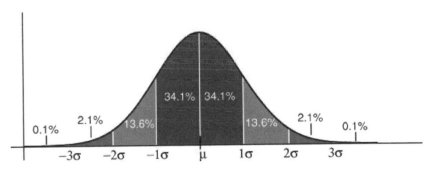

The two parameters that define a normal distribution are the mean (μ, the Greek letter mu) and the standard deviation (σ, the Greek letter sigma). The mean is the built-in AVG() function in SQL. The standard deviation splits the curve into segments of a known size relative to the total population. In pseudocode, the computation for sigma is:

```
SQRT (SUM( POWER (x — AVG(x), 2.0)) / COUNT( * ))
```

Other measurements for this distribution are based on formulas with sigma (σ) and mu (μ). Kurtosis is a measure of how "flat" or "pointy" a distribution is. Skew is a measure of how "tilted to the left or right" a distribution is.

Steve Kass posted the following code on Dejan Sarka's blog for these two calculations, based on a table with an integer age column.

```
SELECT (rx3 - 3*rx2 * av + 3*rx * av*av - rn *
        av * av * av)
        /(POWER(stdv, 3)) * rn /(rn-1) /(rn-2)
        AS age_skew
  FROM (SELECT SUM(age) AS rx,
               SUM(age * age) AS rx2,
               SUM(age * age * age) AS rx3,
               COUNT(age) AS rn,
               STDEV(age) AS stdv,
               AVG(age) AS av
          FROM (SELECT 1e0 * age AS age
                  FROM Personnel)
       ) AS s;
```

and kurtosis:

```
SELECT (rx4 — 4*rx3*av + 6*rx2* av*av — 4* rx*
        av*av*av + rn * POWER(av, 4))
        /(POWER(stdv, 4)) * rn
        * (rn+1) / (rn-1) / (rn-2) / (rn-3)
        - 3e0 * (rn—1) * (rn—1) / (rn—2) / (rn—3)
        AS age_kurt
 FROM (SELECT SUM(age) AS rx,
              SUM(POWER(age, 2)) AS rx2,
              SUM(POWER(age, 3)) AS rx3,
              SUM(POWER(age, 4)) AS rx4,
              COUNT(age) AS rn,
              STDEV(age) AS stdv,
              AVG(age) AS av
         FROM (SELECT 1e0*age AS age — cast it to float
                 FROM Personnel));
```

Steve's original code used repeated multiplication for powers (i.e., (av * av * av * av) = POWER (av, 4). It is important to use the function calls, because we assume (i.e., pray) the compiler writer will correct for floating-point rounding errors.

This is the distribution we expect to find when we do not know of any strong causes to give the data another shape. When you do not have a bell curve, then you can assume that something else is at work.

12.4 Poisson Distribution

Ever stood in a line at a bank? Two factors determine how many people are in that line: how many people arrive in a given time slot and how many people are served by the tellers. The average waiting time is called lambda (λ), and it can be used to compute how many servers (which will reduce the wait time) you need to get a process done in a certain amount of time.

There are classic examples of adjusting a business process based on waiting lines. Many of you are not old enough to remember when bank and airline ticket windows had one line in front of each window. Today, there is one line and the next available teller or reservation clerk services the head of the single line, as defined by red ropes, thanks to mathematicians.

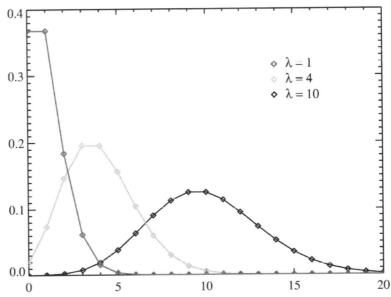

Figure 12.2 Poisson Distributions for average waiting times of 1, 4 and 100

Another variation of the same math was Wal-Mart's promise to open a new checkout line when the line had more than three people waiting. They measured how soon customers would get tired of waiting in a checkout line and abandon their shopping carts.

In the database, the Poisson distribution occurs between the steps of a process. Consider an approval process with multiple steps, and as each application moves from step to step, it queues up after each step.

It is a good idea to have a Poisson distribution model that can flag increases in processing times. The graph is given in Figure 12.2. In the theoretical model, every job or customer will be served in some finite amount of time. In the real world, delay is the deadliest form of denial. Have you ever thought that you would die of old age while on hold on a customer service phone number?

12.5 Logistic or "S" Distribution

The logistic curve has an "S" shape to it. It occurs in fads and things that can be saturated. For example, a new music device comes on the market. Early adopters are few, but people pick up on the trend quickly and the growth shoots up. But at some point, sales slow, because everyone has the product, or there is a replacement for it and your sales level off.

In the real world, the drop in sales is usually the result of a new replacement for the old technology. A classic example is eight-track tapes being replaced by Phillips cassettes, which were in turn replaced by CDs.

12.6 Pareto Distribution

Have you heard of Sturgeon's Revelation (also improperly known as "Sturgeon's Law")? Science fiction writer Theodore Sturgeon wrote in the March 1958 issue of *Venture Science Fiction*: "I repeat Sturgeon's Revelation, which was wrung out of me after 20 years of wearying defense of science fiction against attacks of people who used the worst examples of the field for ammunition, and whose conclusion was that 90 percent of SF is crud." This then was generalized to "90% of everything is crap."

The Pareto principle (also known as the "80-20 rule") is much like Sturgeon's Revelation. It says that 80% of the consequences stem from 20% of the causes. For example, 80% of your profits come from 20% of your customers. It was named after the Italian economist Vilfredo Pareto, who observed that 80% of income went to 20% of the Italian population. The Pareto principle is the basis for the Pareto chart used in Total Quality Control (TQC) and Six Sigma quality control methods.

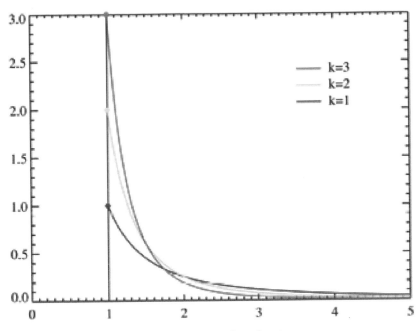

Figure 12.3 Gaussian distribution curve

A version of this kind of phenomena is what Mike Green, CIO of United Pipe, calls the "Sperm Whale" curve (see Figure 12.3). If you look at the cumulative profitability, a few of the most profitable customers quickly account for most of the profitability, and then there is a "bend" in the slope of the curve as we accumulate the typical customers. At the far side of the curve, we start getting the customers who are actually a loss and the curve slopes downward. It looks like the profile of a Sperm Whale—a rising front, sloping back, and a relatively flat middle.

12.7 Distribution Discovery

If you can get a graphics tool, it is often possible to just look at the data and see the most likely kind of distribution it has. But that does not give you a formula that you can use for predictions.

At this point, look for a software tool to help you. Many of the statistical packages will match your data to one of many of these standard distributions automatically. You can also get stand-alone packages designed for PCs or products for mainframes. Some statistical software packages include Abacus Concepts, Domain Solutions, Graph Pad, Jandel Scientific Software, NCSS, RISKview, Stat-Ease, StatSoft, SPSS, and SAS. I suggest that you look at their current offerings on the Internet.

The best place to get such software is to look at software companies that specialize in the science, particularly laboratory analysis. Look at advertisements in *Science* magazine and at Science Online, published by the American Association for the Advancement of Science (AAAS). *Chance* is a magazine jointly published by the American Statistical Association and Springer-Verlag. It is intended for an educated audience with an interest in the analysis of data, so it is not highly mathematical. The Web site is http://www.amstat.org/publications/chance. The articles cover a range of topics from airbag safety to counterterrorism to the authorship of the fifteenth Oz book. It is a great source of ideas.

12.7.1 Missing Data Discovery

You have an expectation when you know something about how data is created. There is a story about a German statistics professor who weighed his bread rations in Nazi Germany and found that the average weight was less than it was supposed to be. He inferred that this meant his baker was using a bread mold that was shorting the customers. When confronted, the baker promised to fix the situation. The professor measured his bread ration again and found that most, but not all, of his rations were at or above the required weight—a skewed distribution! He then went back and found that it was a "ragged right half" of a normal distribution, and the professor determined the actual average weight of the bread had not changed. The baker was simply giving the professor larger pieces. The professor then turned the baker over to the Nazis for fraud.

Many techniques to handle missing data depend on completing a known distribution. The most basic trick is to build a histogram of your data with a graphics tool and then superimpose one of the standard curves over the histogram. The histogram is a bar chart with frequency on the vertical axis and measurements on the horizontal axis. The example given in Figure 12.4 is from the National Weather Service. It shows a time series of UV Index forecasts and actual observations at Boston, Massachusetts. Generally, the UV Index forecast coincides with the observations. For the majority of the forecasts at all sites, the probability of making a correct forecast is quite good. The histogram shows that 26% of the time the UV Index is exactly correct and that 65% of the time the UV Index forecast is within ±1 UV Index unit. And 84% of the time the UV Index is within ±2 UV Index units.

In general, your data will be missing the extreme data because of some natural filtering in your data collection. Assume that credit ratings are normally distributed, ranging from someone with no credit to, say "Joe Celko" at the low end and "Bill Gates" at the high end. Only a few

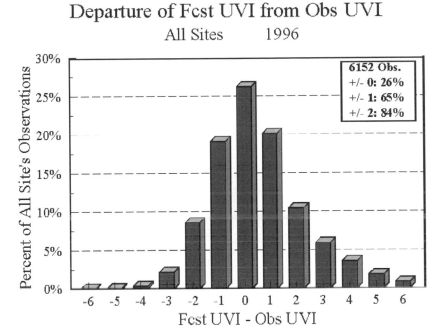

Figure 12.4 Depature of Forecasted UVI from Observed UVI for 1996

businesses will see the whole range of the normal distribution. Marriott Hotels might filter out those people below the "Joe Celko" credit level for their offers. Their data will be "clipped" at the low end. The luxury resorts in the Middle East only see "Bill Gates"–level people in their rooms, so they see only the people five or six standard deviations from the average. The business question is: Can we profitably extend the range of customers from our current customer base? And if we make such a move, how do we know if it worked?

It is more complex than I wish to discuss in a book aimed at database people. You might want to start with *Statistical Analysis with Missing Data* by Roderick J. A. Little and Donald B. Rubin (*Statistical Analysis with Missing Data* [Wiley Series in Probability & Statistics] by Little, Roderick J. and Rubin, Donald B.; ISBN 0471183865, John Wiley, 2002 [second edition]) and Google the current literature.

12.8 References

All illustrations were taken from Wikipedia.com, as well as government sources, which also has good detailed articles on the distributions. The articles also give much more than I have given here.

You can print out several kinds of graph paper from this Web site: http://www.csun.edu/~vceed002/ref/measurement/data/ graph_paper.html

NIST has information and illustrations of various histograms in its engineering statistics handbook Web site: http://www.itl.nist.gov/div898/handbook/eda/gif/histogr0.gif

CHAPTER 13

Market-Basket Analysis

THIS TECHNIQUE LOOKS at collections of things that are somehow related. The usual example is literally a market basket, in which we find that people who have peanut butter also have jelly and bread in their market baskets.

The basket is usually related by one point in time and one "purchaser," but the concept can be generalized to discover interesting (and potentially profitable) correlations. For example, we might find that a purchaser of a new CD player will buy CDs within a week of that purchase, so we stretch the time period. We might find that when Dad buys a new HDTV, the same day the kids buy lots of DVDs, we have extended the purchaser to a family unit.

13.1 Simple Example of a Market Basket

People tend to think that in order to do data mining, you have to be a huge enterprise with a dedicated staff and lots of specialized software. This is simply not true. If I were to tell you that to do gold mining, you had to have a lot of hydraulic equipment and a hundred-person crew, you would know better. If you have the right hole in the ground, you can do quite well with a pick and shovel.

If you watch the Food Network on cable or if you just like Memphis-style BBQ, you know the name "Corky's." The chain was started in 1984 in Memphis by Don Pelts and has grown by franchise at a steady rate ever since. It will never be equivalent to McDonald's, because all the meats are slow cooked for up to 22 hours over hickory wood and charcoal, and then every pork shoulder is hand pulled. There is no automation or mass production.

They sell a small menu of 25 items by mail order via a toll-free number or from their Web site (www.corkysbbq.com) and ship the merchandise in special boxes sometimes using dry ice. Most of the year, their staff can handle the orders. But at Christmas time, they have the problem of meeting the demands created by their success.

Their packing operation consists of two lines. At the start of the line, someone pulls a box of the right size and puts the pick list in it. As it goes down the line, packers put in the items, and when it gets to the end of the line, it is ready for shipment. This is a standard business operation in lots of industries. Their people know what boxes to use for the standard gift packs and can pretty accurately judge any odd-sized orders.

At Christmas time, however, mail-order business is so good that they have to get outside temp help. The temporary help does not have the experience to judge the box sizes by looking at a pick list. If a box that is too small starts down the line, it will jam up things at some point. The supervisor has to get it off the line, and repack the order by hand. If a box that is too large goes down the line, it is a waste of money and creates extra shipping costs. And you do not throw dry ice into any old box, so it needs to be the right kind of box.

Mark Tutt (On the Mark Solutions, LLC) has been consulting with Corky's for years and set up a new order system for them on Sybase. One of the goals of the new system is to print the pick list and shipping labels with all of the calculations done, including which box size the order requires.

Following the rule that you do not reinvent the wheel, Mr. Tutt went to the newsgroups to find out if anyone had a solution already. The suggestions tended to be along the lines of getting the weights and shapes of the items and using a "3D Tetris" program to figure out the packing.

Programmers seem to love to face every new problem as if nobody has ever done it before and nobody will ever do it again. The "code first, research later!" mentality is hard to overcome.

The answer was not in complicated 3D math, but in the past four or five years of orders in the database. People with years of experience had been packing orders and leaving a record of their work to be mined. Obviously, the standard gift packs are easy to spot. But most of the orders tend to be something that had occurred before, too. Here are the answers, if you will bother to dig them out.

First, Mr. Tutt found all of the unique configurations (market baskets) in the orders, how often they occurred, and the boxes used to pack them. If the same configuration had two or more boxes, then you should go with the smallest size. As it turned out, there were about 4,995 unique configurations in the custom orders, which covered about 99.5% of the cases. The remaining 0.5% is flagged as a "hand pick" job to be handled by a supervisor.

Now, let's show some actual SQL code.

13.2 Relational Division

Relational division is one of the least known and applied of the eight basic operations in Codd's relational algebra. The idea is that a divisor table is used to partition a dividend table and produce a quotient or results table. The quotient table is made up of those values of one column for which a second column had all of the values in the divisor.

This is easier to explain with an example. We have a table of customers and the products they bought (dividend); we have a table of products in the basket we are researching (divisor); we want the names of the customers who bought every product (quotient) in the basket. To get this result, we divide the purchases table by the products in the basket.

```
CREATE TABLE Purchases
(customer_id CHAR(15) NOT NULL,
 product_code CHAR(15) NOT NULL,
 PRIMARY KEY (customer_id, product_code));
```

```
Purchases
customer      product_code
=========================
'Celko'       'Apples'
'Higgins'     'Oranges'
'Higgins'     'Butter'
'Higgins'     'Apples'
'Jones'       'Oranges'
```

```
'Jones'    'Butter'
'Smith'    'Bread'
'Smith'    'Oranges'
'Smith'    'Butter'
'Wilson'   'Bread'
'Wilson'   'Oranges'
'Wilson'   'Butter'
'Wilson'   'Fish'
```

```
CREATE TABLE Basket
(product_code CHAR(15) NOT NULL PRIMARY KEY);
```

```
Basket
Product_code
==========
'Bread'
'Oranges'
'Butter'
```

```
Purchases DIVIDED BY Basket
Customer_id
=============================
'Smith'
'Wilson'
```

In this example, Smith and Wilson are the two customers who bought everything in the basket. Notice that Higgins and Celko buy apples, but we don't have one in the basket. In Codd's original definition of relational division, having more rows than are called for is not a problem.

The important characteristic of a relational division is that the CROSS JOIN of the divisor and the quotient produces a valid subset of rows from the dividend. This is where the name comes from, since the CROSS JOIN acts like a multiplication operator.

13.2.1 Division with a Remainder

There are two kinds of relational division. Division with a remainder allows the dividend table to have more values than the divisor, which was Dr. Codd's original definition. For example, if a customer bought more products than just those that we have in the basket, this is fine with us. The query can be written as:

```
SELECT DISTINCT customer_id
  FROM Purchases AS P1
 WHERE NOT EXISTS()
       (SELECT *
          FROM Basket
         WHERE NOT EXISTS()
               (SELECT *
                  FROM Purchases AS P2
                 WHERE (P1.customer_id = P2.customer_id)
                   AND (P2.product_code = Basket.product_code)));
```

The quickest way to explain this is to word it as, "There ain't no product in this basket that Mr. X has not bought!" While it is poor English, it is valid logic. This query for relational division was made popular by Chris Date in his textbooks, but it is neither the only method nor always the fastest. Another version of the division can be written so as to avoid three levels of nesting. While it is not original with me, I have made it popular in my books.

```
SELECT P1.customer_id
  FROM Purchases AS P1, Basket AS B1
 WHERE P1.product_code = B1.product_code
 GROUP BY P1.customer_id
HAVING COUNT(P1.product_code)
     = (SELECT COUNT(product_code) FROM Basket);
```

There is a serious difference in the two methods. Dump the basket, so that the divisor is empty. Because of the NOT EXISTS() predicates in Date's query, all customers are returned from a division by an empty set. Because of the COUNT() functions in my query, no customers are returned from a division by an empty set.

In the sixth edition of his book, *An Introduction to Database Systems*, 6th Edition by C. J. Date: ISBN 0-201-56341-X, Addison-Wesley, 1995, Chris Date defined another operator (DIVIDEBY . . . PER) that produces the same results as my query, but with more complexity.

13.2.2 Exact Division

The second kind of relational division is exact relational division. The dividend table must match exactly to the values of the divisor without any extra values.

```
SELECT P1.customer_id
  FROM Purchases AS P1
       LEFT OUTER JOIN
       Basket AS B1
       ON P1.product_code = B1.product_code
 GROUP BY P1.customer_id
HAVING COUNT(P1.product_code)
       = (SELECT COUNT(product_code) FROM Basket)
   AND COUNT(B1.product_code)
       = (SELECT COUNT(product_code) FROM Basket);
```

This says that a customer must have the same number of purchases as there are products in the basket, and these purchases must all match to a product in the basket, not something else. The "something else" is shown by a created NULL from the LEFT OUTER JOIN.

13.2.3 Todd's Division

A relational division operator proposed by Stephen Todd is defined on two tables with common columns that are joined together, dropping the JOIN column and retaining only those non-JOIN columns that meet a criterion.

We are given a table, JobParts(job_nbr, part_nbr), and another table, SupParts(sup_nbr, part_nbr), of suppliers and the parts that they provide. We want to get the supplier-and-job pairs such that supplier sn supplies all of the parts needed for job jn. This is not quite the same thing as getting the supplier-and-job pairs such that job jn requires all of the parts provided by supplier sn.

You want to divide the JobParts table by the SupParts table. A general rule is that the remainder comes from the dividend, but all values in the divisor are present.

```
JobParts         SupParts           Result = JobSups
job pno          sno   pno          job sno
========         ==============     ============
'j1'  'p1'       's1'   'p1'          'j1'  's1'
'j1'  'p2'       's1'   'p2'          'j1'  's2'
'j2'  'p2'       's1'   'p3'          'j2'  's1'
'j2'  'p4'       's1'   'p4'          'j2'  's4'
'j2'  'p5'       's1'   'p5'          'j3'  's1'
'j3'  'p2'       's1'   'p6'          'j3'  's2'
                 's2'   'p1'          'j3'  's3'
```

```
        's2'    'p2'              'j3'   's4'
        's3'    'p2'
        's4'    'p2'
        's4'    'p4'
        's4'    'p5'
```

Pierre Mullin submitted the following query to carry out the Todd division:

```
SELECT DISTINCT JP1.job, SP1.supplier
  FROM JobParts AS JP1, SupParts AS SP1
 WHERE NOT EXISTS()
       (SELECT *
          FROM JobParts AS JP2
         WHERE JP2.job = JP1.job
           AND JP2.part
               NOT IN
               (SELECT SP2.part
                  FROM SupParts AS SP2
                 WHERE SP2.supplier = SP1.supplier));
```

This is really a modification of the query for Codd's division, extended to use a JOIN on both tables in the outermost SELECT statement. The IN() predicate for the second subquery can be replaced with a NOT EXISTS() predicate; it might run a bit faster, depending on the optimizer.

Another related query is finding the pairs of suppliers who sell the same parts. In this data, that would be the pairs (s1, p2), (s3, p1), (s4, p1), and (s5, p1).

```
SELECT S1.sup, S2.sup
  FROM SupParts AS S1, SupParts AS S2
 WHERE S1.sup < S2.sup      -- different suppliers
   AND S1.part = S2.part  -- same parts
 GROUP BY S1.sup, S2.sup
HAVING COUNT(*)
       = (SELECT COUNT (*)  -- same count of parts
                  FROM SupParts AS S3
                 WHERE S3.sup = S1.sup)
   AND COUNT(*) = (SELECT COUNT (*)
                  FROM SupParts AS S4
                 WHERE S4.sup = S2.sup);
```

This can be modified easily into Todd's division by adding the restriction that the parts must also belong to a common job.

13.2.4 Division with Set Operators

The standard SQL set difference operator, EXCEPT, can be used to write a very compact version of Dr. Codd's relational division. The EXCEPT operator removes the divisor set from the dividend set. If the result is empty, we have a match; if there is anything left over, it has failed. Using the purchases and basket example, we would write:

```
SELECT DISTINCT customer_id
  FROM Purchases AS P1
 WHERE (SELECT product_code FROM Basket
        EXCEPT
        SELECT product_code
          FROM Purchases AS P2
         WHERE P1.customer_id = P2.customer_id) IS NULL;
```

Again, informally, you can imagine that we received a purchase list from each customer, walked over to the basket, and crossed off each product he or she bought. If we marked off all the products in the basket, we would keep this customer. Another trick is that an empty subquery expression returns a NULL, which is how we can test for an empty set. The WHERE clause could just as well have used a NOT EXISTS() predicate instead of the IS NULL predicate.

13.3 Romney's Division

This somewhat complicated relational division is due to Richard Romley at Salomon Smith Barney. The original problem deals with two tables. The first table has a list of managers and the projects they can manage. The second table has a list of personnel, their departments, and the project to which they are assigned. Each employee is assigned to one and only one department, and each employee works on one and only one project at a time. But a department can have several different projects at the same time, so a single project can span several departments.

```
CREATE TABLE MgrProjects
(mgr_name CHAR(10) NOT NULL,
 project_id CHAR(2) NOT NULL,
 PRIMARY KEY(mgr_name, project_id));
```

```
INSERT INTO Mgr_Project
VALUES ('M1', 'P1'), ('M1', 'P3'),
       ('M2', 'P2'), ('M2', 'P3'),
       ('M3', 'P2'),
       ('M4', 'P1'), ('M4', 'P2'), ('M4', 'P3');

CREATE TABLE Personnel
(emp_id CHAR(10) NOT NULL,
 dept CHAR(2) NOT NULL,
 project_id CHAR(2) NOT NULL,
 UNIQUE (emp_id, project_id),
 UNIQUE (emp_id, dept),
 PRIMARY KEY (emp_id, dept, project_id));

-- load department #1 data
INSERT INTO Personnel
VALUES ('Al', 'D1', 'P1'),
       ('Bob', 'D1', 'P1'),
       ('Carl', 'D1', 'P1'),
       ('Don', 'D1', 'P2'),
       ('Ed', 'D1', 'P2'),
       ('Frank', 'D1', 'P2'),
       ('George', 'D1', 'P2');

-- load department #2 data
INSERT INTO Personnel
VALUES ('Harry', 'D2', 'P2'),
       ('Jack', 'D2', 'P2'),
       ('Larry', 'D2', 'P2'),
       ('Mike', 'D2', 'P2'),
       ('Nat', 'D2', 'P2');

-- load department #3 data
INSERT INTO Personnel
VALUES ('Oscar', 'D3', 'P2'),
       ('Pat', 'D3', 'P2'),
       ('Rich', 'D3', 'P3');
```

The problem is to generate a report showing each manager for each department and whether he or she is qualified to manage none, some, or all of the projects being worked on within the department.

This query uses a characteristic function, while my original version compares a count of personnel under each manager to a count of personnel under each project_id. The use of "GROUP BY M1.mgr_name, P1.dept_name, P2.project_id" with the "SELECT DISTINCT M1.mgr_name, P1.dept_name" is really the tricky part in this new query. What we have is a three-dimensional space with the (x, y, z) axis representing (mgr_name, dept_name, project_id), and then we reduce it to two dimensions (mgr_name, dept) by seeing if personnel on shared project_ids cover the department or not.

That observation leads to the next changes. We can build a table that shows each combination of manager, department, and the level of authority they have over the projects they have in common. That is the derived table T1 in the following query; (authority = 1) means the manager is not on the project and authority = 2 means that he or she is on the project_id.

```
SELECT T1.mgr_name, T1.dept_name,
       CASE SUM(T1.authority)
       WHEN 1 THEN 'None'
       WHEN 2 THEN 'All'
       WHEN 3 THEN 'Some'
       ELSE NULL END AS power
  FROM (SELECT DISTINCT M1.mgr_name, P1.dept_name,
               MAX (CASE WHEN M1.project_id = P1.project_id
                        THEN 2 ELSE 1 END) AS authority
          FROM MgrProjects AS M1
               CROSS JOIN
               Personnel AS P1
         GROUP BY m.mgr_name, P1.dept_name, P1.project_id) AS T1
 GROUP BY T1.mgr_name, T1.dept_name;
```

Another version, using the basket example:

```
SELECT P1.customer_id,
       CASE WHEN COUNT(P1.product_code) > (SELECT
COUNT(product_code) FROM Basket)
               AND COUNT(B1.product_code) = (SELECT
COUNT(product_code)FROM Basket)
           THEN 'more than all'
           WHEN COUNT(P1.product_code) = (SELECT
COUNT(product_code) FROM Basket)
```

```
                        AND COUNT(B1.product_code) = (SELECT
COUNT(product_code) FROM Basket)
              THEN 'exactly all  '
              WHEN MIN(B1.product_code) IS NULL
              THEN 'none            '
              ELSE 'some            ' END AS purchase_lvl
    FROM Purchases AS P1
         LEFT OUTER JOIN
         Basket AS B1
         ON P1.product_code = B1.product_code
    GROUP BY P1.customer_id;
```

We can now sum the authority numbers for all the projects within a department to determine the power this manager has over the department as a whole. If he or she has a total of one, he or she has no authority over personnel on any project in the department. If the manager has a total of two, he or she has power over all personnel on all projects in the department. If he or she has a total of three, this manager has both a 1 and a 2 authority total on some projects within the department. Here is the final answer.

```
Results
mgr_name dept power
====================--

   M1   D1   Some
   M1   D2   None
   M1   D3   Some
   M2   D1   Some
   M2   D2   All
   M2   D3   All
   M3   D1   Some
   M3   D2   All
   M3   D3   Some
   M4   D1   All
   M4   D2   All
   M4   D3   All
```

13.4 How to Use Relational Divisions

You have no choice about the dividend; it is going to be a fact table. But you do have a choice about the divisor. Remember that every n-item basket is also an (n−1) basket, an (n−2) basket, and so forth. The temptation is to start with a large basket and then pull out an interesting subset. It is better to start with a "reasonable guess" as to the basket and test for it first. The problem is that relational division can be slow to execute as the divisor gets larger.

A general rule is that your "market basket" should have fewer than five items. As an actual example from the grocery industry, consider looking for baskets that have your product and magazines. The business question is to find which magazines users of your product buy so you know which advertisements worked. Then ask the next question: Which magazines do people who do not buy your product, but use a competitor's product, read? This tells you where to place advertisements and coupons to get them to switch.

CHAPTER 14

Decision, Classification, and Regression Trees

ONE THING WE will want to do with data is build hierarchical classification schemes that give us rules for handling the data. Either we have a "bucket" to file it in or we have some predictions we can make. Several methods for modeling tree structures in SQL are available in my book *Joe Celko's Trees and Hierarchies in SQL for Smarties* by Joe Celko; ISBN 1-55860-920-2, Morgan_Kaufmann, 2004, which can be used to store the results of the following methods so they can be used in queries.

Regression assumes that we can fit real data into a (simple) formula to obtain an accurate prediction of future data. The usual example is linear regression, which we have already discussed. The branching in the tree is determined by a regression formula.

Classification trees have their rules set without the use of a formula. Many times, they are set by law, industry standards, or regulations. Drug classification is an example of law, standards, and regulations being applied at once.

Decision trees also have rules, but their goal is to select an action. You will probably use them for data scrubbing. They all get grouped together because they are similar in structure and results. But let's start with a simple tool.

14.1 Casual Caldistics

I want to apologize for the title of this section, but I want to use a classification system example that most people are aware of from high school. Biologists look at DNA chains, genes, and physical characteristics to determine the path of evolution from one species to another. The math, chemical, and structural analysis used in this field are actually complex, but this popularized version will give you some basic ideas.

The first person to attempt to set up a classification system for animals was Aristotle, and his system stayed in place until the seventeenth century. A Swede named Carolus Linnaeus improved on Aristotle's system and introduced the method we now use to name species. In the Linnaean method, there are kingdoms of life at the top of the hierarchy, then a family includes one or more genera. A genus contains one or more species, and the species have two-part Latin names.

Linnaeus's system stayed in place until 1950, when Willi Henning invented caldistics. The assumption in caldistics is that two animals that share a large number of characteristics evolved from a common ancestor. The two animals branched off from this ancestor based on the characteristics by which they differ.

Linnaeus guessed there were fewer than 15,000 species of animals and plants on earth. Today, we have names for 1.5 to 2.0 million species and are still adding names. Strangely, no complete database of names exists right now. But several projects are underway.

What does this have to do with databases and commercial applications? You can use the techniques to derive classifications for other data. Instead of animals, we could look at, say, customers and build a cladogram. A cladogram is a binary tree that ends with the "species" on the leaf nodes. The nonleaf nodes are determined by hypotheses of a common ancestor. Different hypotheses lead to different trees, so it is difficult to say that one cladogram is correct.

As an example, let's look at customers who buy peanut butter, jelly, sliced meat, and bread when they shop. One hypothesis is that the peanut butter and jelly buyers are species of some common kind of customer, say people with younger children; likewise, sliced meat and bread buyers are species of brown baggers (see Figure 14.1).

Another hypothesis is that the bread and jelly buyers have something in common, while peanut butter and sliced meat have no strong relationship with anything in the set (see Figure 14.2).

Why use a cladogram? The cladogram lets you pick which attributes to consider and play with the configuration. This is not a statistical tool

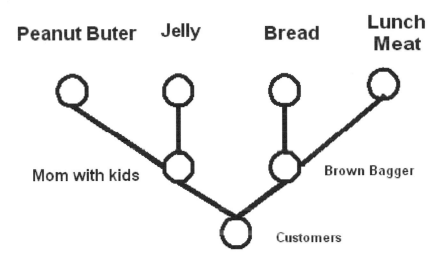

Figure 14.1 Market Basket Clade #1

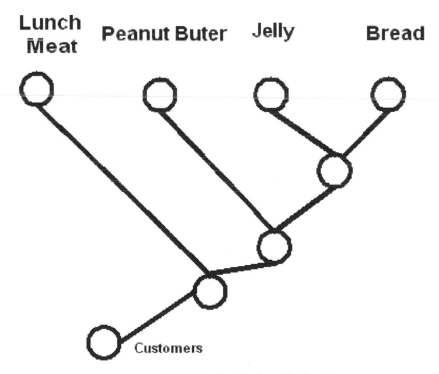

Figure 14.2 Market Basket Clade #2

as presented, but a "mind tool" to get you started. Now, let's go to heavier math.

14.2 Decision and Correlation Trees

Let's start with a table full of data about medical information and lifestyle habits on people (Figure 14.3). We want to find the a rule that predicts one of the attributes (dependent variable), such as high blood pressure, from the other attributes (independent variables), such as eating habits, smoking, drinking, age, and so forth.

The set of rules will be a hierarchy that lets us travel from the root to a leaf node to classify a new patient by taking measurements and asking questions. Assume that the strongest predictor of high blood pressure is age—older people are more likely to have high blood pressure than younger people. This is the fist level of the rule set.

Within the subset of younger people with high blood pressure, what makes them different from their peer group? We repeat the process on just the "younger people" subset and find that younger people who smoke and drink too much have high blood pressure. But let's also look at older people with the same process. And we discover that older people who survived booze and cigarettes in their youth are now menaced by salt and fatty food in their diet.

We can continue the process with the subsets of "younger people who smoke and drink too much," "younger people who do not smoke and drink," "older people who eat poorly," and "older people who eat properly" for as many levels of attributes as we have.

Yes is to the left and No is to the right

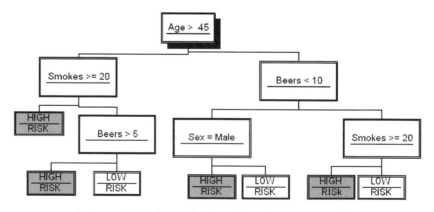

Figure 14.3 Classification Tree for Living Habits

Most classification techniques assume that there is one dependent variable that we wish to predict (e.g., high blood pressure or purchase of a product) and that everything else is a potential "predictor" variable of various strength (e.g., age is a strong predictor of high blood pressure, but newspaper subscriptions are not).

Dependent or predictor variables are either categorical values (i.e., a single discrete value like "male" or "female") or continuous values (i.e., age), which have to be converted to ranges (i.e., "kid" means "between 1 and 19," "young" means 20–35, middle aged means 36–50, and "old" is 51–99 years of age, or whatever the data supports).

What we want to get out of the data is a decision tree with branches that we can follow based on the test at each node. These trees can use a different confidence level at each level; they are, therefore, not parametric. Parametric models require a specific kind of rule, such as a linear function, that you probably do not know in advance.

Another advantage is that the statistical package picks the required variables based on math, rather than a wild guess. Furthermore, you do not need to do linear transforms on the data for this to work; with other tools, you might have to do a logarithmic transformation.

One of the more interesting results is that the same attribute can appear in more than one path. For example, you might find that younger people and older people who eat too much salt are in trouble, but middle-aged people are not. Outliers are not a problem, and you can use dummy values for missing values.

Each group is partitioned independently of all others, and you can keep going as long as you have data. In theory, you could reduce any single row of data to a horrible, long rule. This would become a bush instead of a tree, and each branch would be so specific that it would be useless in the real world.

Figure 14.3 gives you an idea of a classification tree for a person who is at a high or low health risk. This is a fictitious example, so do not worry what the numbers mean or whether or not the data makes sense. The predictors are "smoking," "alcohol consumption," "gender," and "age"; note that gender is the only categorical value in this example. We need to have some idea what the noncategorical scales are, so let's assume that we use cigarettes per day, cans of beer per day, and age in whole years.

The first split is on age—we find more high-risk people who are older than 45 than high-risk younger people. Next, let's follow down each branch. Older people who smoke more than 20 cigarettes per day are exclusively high risk, and older nonsmokers need to watch their drinking and keep it under 5 cans of beer per day.

But when do we stop? It depends on both how detailed a rule we want and the quality of the sample data from which we built the rule. We seek a balance of x% accuracy against a perfect classification for the current data that will probably fail with new data. We want to pick the branching based on how much information each attribute gives us. That gets us to entropy.

14.3 Entropy

Entropy is the measurement of information content of a message. At one extreme, a message has zero content if we already know something. For example, imagine a room full of people. Just asking whether anyone in the room is over 15 feet tall has no information value because we know that the answer is always "no," so we do not have to ask it. At the other extreme, if I ask whether anyone is over 1 foot tall, we know the answer is always "yes," so we do not need to ask the question. If we know someone's name, DNA and fingerprints, we can go directly to that one person. All those identifiers carry a lot of information and the odds of errors in all three is astronomical.

Somewhere in between, we can have questions that give us various levels of information. The formula we use from information theory uses log2() and returns a value in bits. If you have forgotten your high school algebra, the formula is $\log2(x) = \log(x)/\log(2.0)$ to convert from the natural logorithm to the base two logorithm.

The formula for a question with (n) possible options is the summation of the entropy of each probability.

```
Entropy (p1, p2, .., pn) =  i (-pi * log2(pi))
```

The negative sign will guarantee that the answer is always equal to or greater than zero. The probabilities will always total to one. For example, assume that we have an attribute for sales volume that is scaled as "high" with 2 cases, "medium" with 3 cases, and "low" with 4 cases, and a table containing that data:

```
CREATE TABLE SalesExample
(sales_vol_code CHAR(3) NOT NULL PRIMARY KEY
        CHECK (sales_vol_code IN ('low', 'med', 'hi ')),
  occurs INTEGER NOT NULL
```

```
CHECK (occurs > 0));

INSERT INTO SalesExample VALUES ('low', 2);
INSERT INTO SalesExample VALUES ('med', 3);
INSERT INTO SalesExample VALUES ('hi ', 4);
```

It is handy to have the probabilities for each value of an attribute, so I would construct a VIEW or derived table, as shown here.

```
SELECT SUM(-prob *(LOG(prob)/ 0.69314718055994529))
  FROM (SELECT sales_vol_code, occurs,
          occurs /(SELECT SUM(occurs * 1.0)
                  FROM SalesExample)
        AS Probabilities (sales_vol_code, occurs, prob);
```

The negative sign will guarantee that the answer is always equal to or greater than zero. The probabilities will always total to one. In this example, knowing the sales volume is worth ~1.530 bits. By comparing its bit score to the other attributes, you can design a decision tree. Start with the attribute that gives the most information on average and put it at the root; then continue the same process in each subgroup.

14.4 Other Algorithms and Software

You can get several free tree packages in UNIX, Windows, and Macintosh versions from the statistics department at the University of Wisconsin (http://www.stat.wisc.edu/~loh). Most of the work on these packages has been done by Wei-Yin Loh (University of Wisconsin–Madison) and Yu-Shan Shih (National Chung Cheng University, Taiwan).

QUEST stands for quick, unbiased, and efficient statistical tree. It is similar to the CART algorithm given in "Classification and Regression Trees by Leo Breiman; ISBN 0412048418, Chapman & Hall/CRC, 1984. QUEST is generally faster than CART or chi-squared automatic interaction detector (CHAID), but it needs more main storage. This is fine for smaller data sets, but not so good for larger data sets.

Classification rule with unbiased interaction selection and estimation (CRUISE) was developed by Hyunjoong Kim (Yonsei University, Korea) and Wei-Yin Loh (University of Wisconsin–Madison). It is an improved descendant of an older algorithm called FACT (Factor Analysis Tree).

Generalized, unbiased, interaction detection and estimation (GUIDE) is a multipurpose machine learning algorithm for constructing regression trees. It has options for adjusting how the splits are made and how missing values are handled.

Angoss Software (http://www.angoss.com) sells KnowledgeSeeker and other products for this kind of work. It is based on a Bonferroni tree algorithm.

CART is a registered trademark of California Statistical Software. CART is technically known as a binary recursive partitioning of data, since it uses a two-way split at each partition decision. It is the simplest member of a family of techniques that involve regression statistics hidden in the software. Other techniques split along two or more subsets and usually have a confidence level; this means that the data says that "x% of time, age is tied to high blood pressure" by some relationship. The value of x can vary; if you are exploring data, you might use 75% confidence, but if you are trying to get a rule for medical work, you might want to be 95% or 98% certain of your rules.

CHAID was invented in the 1980s when computer power was becoming inexpensive. Like CART, it builds trees, but they are nonbinary and work well with larger amounts of data. One advantage for market research is that data is broken into multiple categories near the root, so you can quickly see market segment.

The basic algorithm relies on a Chi-square for categorical data or an F-test for continuous data test for each split. The process requires a few passes over the data.

First, the continuous attributes have to be put into categories of approximately equal size. The categorical data is ready as it stands. The second step is to find out whether any categories can be merged together, because there is no significant difference in how they predict the dependent value. Usually, these data ranges will be contiguous. This is where the chi-square test is used on a continuous dependent variable or an F test is used on a categorical dependent variable.

At this point, the values are adjusted with a Bonferroni p-value for the set of categories we have found. Without going into the math, the smallest Bonferroni adjusted p-value determines that we have arrived at a terminal node in the tree.

If you wish, you can use more complex algorithms. There is a family of algorithms called *exhaustive CHAID*, which basically keeps running until it has only two categories for each independent data element. This gives the most significant split for that subset of data. However, this gets to be expensive as you add more variables.

Another problem is that your trees can be too deep, too wide, or complex for a human being to use. We are not able to process more than about five to seven parameters in a problem. At some point, you have to trim the tree.

CHAPTER
15

Computer-Intensive Analysis

O NE OF THE reasons traditonal statistics evolved as it did was that the computations required to large amounts of data simply could not be done before computers. It was easier to assume thigns about the data instead of actually looking at it in detail. Imagine a room full of people with mechanitcal calculators in front of them, each performing a step in an algorithm and combining their result by hand onto ledger sheets. When Computers got chepacr, statistical packages were possible. But teh packages were still based on the older methods that had begun with manual computations. We merely automated that room of clerks. As the trend to cheaper and cheaper hardware (aka "Moore's law") continued, other possible ways of doing statistics became possible.

Resampling is a family of statistics techniques that are only possible with big-cheap computer power. Instead of assuming that we know the statistical distribution (this is called parametric statistics), we discover what is in the actual data by taking samples from it. A nonparametric statistic is based on tests on the data at hand. Resampling and nonparametrics let us analyze strange or skewed data that does not follow formulas.

The principal proponent of the technique was the late Julian Simon, the economist who first proposed that airlines offer to reward passengers who were overbooked for taking a later flight.

Julian Simon and Paul Ehrlich (butterfly expert and author of *The Population Bomb* by Paul R. Ehrlich; ISBN 1568495870, Buccaneer Books (Reprint edition), 1995 and a whole raft of other doomsday books that have all been proven wrong) made a bet in 1980. They took an imaginary $1,000 and let Ehrlich pick commodities. The bet was that the real prices would go up or down in the next 10 years as an objective, measurable reflection of the state of the world. If the real costs went down, then Simon would collect the real difference adjusted to then-current dollars; if the real costs went up, then Ehrlich would collect the difference adjusted to then-current dollars.

Ehrlich picked metals: copper, chrome, nickel, tin, and tungsten and "invested" $200 in each. In 1990, Ehrlich paid Simon $576.07 and did not call one of his usual press conferences about it. What was even funnier is that if Ehrlich had paid off in then-current dollars, not adjusted for inflation, he would still have lost!

Julian Simon then got involved with resampling statistics at the University of Maryland, wrote books on it, and designed a training package complete with a simple 20-statement teaching programming language.

The advantage of such techniques in business applications is that the data mining world is very often nonparametric. The population is often a "work in progress," rather than a neatly packaged, completed whole.

15.1 Bootstraps

Bootstrapping is a technique created by Bradley Efron ("Computer Intensive Methods in Statistics," *Scientific American*, May 1991, pp. 116–130). Briefly stated, when given a small sample, we can make multiple copies of the data and put them into the sample until we get a usable size.

The idea is that each sample will behave "something like" the population. If the samples vary too much, then the data might be "too strange" to find any useful pattern. You are simulating scenarios from the data you have, under the assumption that your samples reflect the population from which they were drawn.

15.2 Subgroups

To use an example from an article by Julian Simon and Peter Bruce in *Chance* (Vol. 4, No. 1, 1991), assume you are given the 1961 price of a fifth of Seagram 7 Crown whiskey for 16 states that have state-monopolized liquor stores and for 26 states that have privately owned liquor stores. The average price for the monopoly states is $4.35, and it is $4.84 in the free-market states. Is this difference due to the monopoly or due to chance?

This kind of problem is usually handled with a Student's *t* test. The test was developed by W. S. Gosset, a chemist working at the Guinness Brewery in Dublin for industrial processes. The company asked him to publish under the pen name "Student"—hence the name of the test. The t-test takes two independent samples of the same size, pairs up their data points and compares the differences. When the samples are not the same size, you can make some adjustments and still use it. But in fact, there is no good justification for using it because it was designed for relatively small samples and assumes things about the differences in measurements.

The resampling approach makes no assumptions about the distributions. Instead, imagine that you put all 42 prices on a deck of cards. You then shuffle the deck and draw samples of 16 and 26 cards over and over. Do it hundreds of times or thousands of times. For each sample, you take the two averages. We then make a histogram of the differences and look at it. In the actual sample, there was a difference of $0.49; thus, anytime we go over that number, we can say "Yes, the price difference was due to chance" and when it goes below $0.49, we can say "No, there is a monopoly effect." And, in case you are interested, there was no monopoly effect.

The only assumption is that all prices are equally likely to be picked from the deck. But notice that you can change that assumption easily with resampling when you have more attributes to consider. For example, a person who bought jelly in the last week is more likely to be in the subset of peanut butter buyers than non peanut butter buyers.

15.3 Bayesian Analysis

Bayesian statistics is based on the idea that the best predictor of future or current behavior is past behavior. Resampling is very useful for this kind of analysis, because all you do is set up a simulation, rather than bother with formulas.

The most popular example of how people can be fooled by a Bayesian problem is the "Monty Hall problem," which is based on a once-popular television quiz program. The contestant is shown three doors (A, B, C). Two of the doors have a wet goat behind them, and only one has an automobile. He or she then picks one of the doors to win the prize. But wait! Monty stops the game, and opens one of the other doors (which has one of the wet goats behind it). Now, the contestant is asked if he wants to keep the door he picked or a switch to the remaining unopened door.

Should you switch or does it matter? It matters; you double your chances by switching. Almost everyone, including mathematicians, thinks that it does not matter. If you run a simulation, you will see the answer immediately.

The logic is that your first choice is drawn from a population of 3, so your odds of finding the car are 33.33% or 1/3. Monty does not open the door with the automobile when he sets up the second drawing.

	A	B	C
1	Goat	Goat	Automobile
2	Goat	Automobile	Goat
3	Automobile	Goat	Goat

Let's assume you choose door A, and we do not know if we are playing with arrangement 1, 2, or 3. Now Monthy throws away one of the "goat doors" for you. In cases 1 and 2, he eliminates doors B and C, respectively, since they are the only remaining goat doors. If you switch, you win in cases 1 and 2, so your odds are now 2/3 of winning and not 1/3.

One of the classic Bayesian problems involves false positives in a test for a disease. Assume the disease occurs in 1 person per 1,000 persons in the population. Our test gives us a false positive 5% of the time in those people we test. The question is, "What are the odds that Mr. X with a positive result actually has the disease?"

We could do this with Bayesian formulas, but let us define a simulation instead. We start with a sample of 1,000 cases, of which one is a false positive. (Notice we are not bothering with false negatives). This simulates the whole population.

If I pick the false positive, the trial is over; if I pick a true positive case, I pull out another sample, which has 95 positives and 5 false positives. Repeat these trial simulations a few thousand times and discover the ratio of true positives to false positives. When Cascells, Schoenberger, and Grayboys ("Interpretation by Physicians of Clinical Laboratory Studies," *New England Journal of Medicine*, Vol. 229, pp. 999–1000) presented this problem to Harvard medical students and teachers, almost half of them guessed 95%, which is horribly wrong.

This example is a probability calculation using nice round, known probabilities that came out of the textbook. But what if we have no idea as to what numbers really are? Census data can often provide an idea of the total population. And we know something about the ratios we get in our own data. While it will not be exact, you can use this data to estimate the number of potential customers that you have not contacted yet.

15.4 Clustering

Imagine that you live in a large city and you want to open a few neighborhood pubs. Let's say that you do a survey and find out which households are British, Irish, German, and so forth, and how much they drink. You take your survey and go to your map with colored pushpins for each ethnic group. You look at the pins and try to see clusters of pins—the areas where your clients will be found. Within each cluster, you try the most central location for your various pubs.

This is the general idea behind *k-means clustering*. You start with a hypothesis about the number of clusters (k) you want, and you try to put them into that number of clusters that are as distinct as possible. In this example, (k) will be the number of pubs you can afford to open. My guess is that there is room in this city for a British pub, a German Rathskeller, and a yuppie Fern Bar. The clientele will not be very much alike.

I start with my surveys and put them in (k) random clusters; then I move people between those clusters so as to minimize variability within clusters and maximize variability between clusters. My similarity rules might include clothing as one rule, so I move anyone who wears a lot of tweed to the British cluster, anyone who wears lederhosen to the German cluster, and anyone wearing Armani suits to the Yuppie cluster. But it is better to use continuous measurements instead of categories—say, gallons of beer and wine consumed per year for each household.

We examine the mean values on each dimension to determine how distinct our (k) clusters are. If we are lucky, we will have very different means for most (but probably not all) dimensions in the data. Within each cluster, we would like the variance to be low. We are looking for tight islands of data—say, a "Germantown" section of the city that can support a Rathskeller.

15.4.1 Uses for Clustering

The k-means clustering methods are used for neural networks, image processing, pattern recognition, artificial intelligent, and so forth. It generally works well for problems that have these islands of similar data.

In data mining applications, we have two basic approaches. We can compute the clusters once and use them to classify the new data. A better approach is to recompute the clusters at regular intervals. Thus, we might find that the Germans are not wearing Lederhosen as much as they used to, and it is no longer a strong predictor. This kind of population shift can be important over time.

15.4.2 Problems with Clustering

It should be obvious that when (k =1), we will be centered on the mean of the attributes, and we have gained nothing. If we guess a value of (k) that is too low, we will get too much variance in the clusters to be useful. In my example, (k = 2) might lump Brits and yuppies together, because they are more like each other and less like Germans. If the (k) value is set too high, I can get clusters that overlap and do not really put things into useful distinct clusters. For example, breaking my yuppies into BMW drivers and Lexis drivers is not a big help.

A bad guess for the starting clusters can result in a lot of computing time trying to fit the data into buckets. A smaller data set will form clusters that are highly dependent on the initial guesses for the centroids. Hopefully, we can make good guesses at the extremes—we already have an idea about who is a yuppie and who goes to a biker bar.

Some algorithms can take the same data in a different order and produce a slightly different cluster. This is the result of a local optimum. Again, sticking to the pubs example, imagine that you find a bar you like near to your house. You continue to go there, never even looking for a new bar that might be a better fit for you.

Another factor is that we don't know which attribute contributes more to the clustering process, since we assume that each attribute has the same weight. We can add weights to the values, but that can be tricky and time consuming.

The mean is not a good measure of central tendency when we have outliers. One German who lives far from Germantown distorts the average travel distance to my Rathskeller. The median would be a better statistic if we have that situation, or we might want to throw out the outliers.

The clusters will have a "circular" shape, because they are based on a simple distance formula. What if they should be ovals? Again, with the pubs example, what if Germantown is laid out on one main street that runs for many blocks?

There are a lot of free clustering programs available on the Internet, and most statistical packages will have one or more routines.

Do not confuse clustering and classification. Classifications exist a priori, and you put things into categories. Clustering finds groupings in the data; it can be used to set up classification schemes.

CHAPTER 16

Relationship Analytics

"**S**IX DEGREES FROM Kevin Bacon" is a popular game that started at Albright College in Reading, Pennsylvania, and was made popular on Jon Stewart's first show on MTV. The idea is that Kevin Bacon can be linked with any other actor in the world via movie appearances. For example, Jack Nicholson was in *A Few Good Men* with Kevin Bacon. Michelle Pfeiffer was in *Wolf* with Jack Nicholson, who was in *A Few Good Men* with Kevin Bacon. The number of links is your "Bacon number," which cannot be greater than six—B(Nicholson) = 1, B(Pfeiffer) = 2 and B(Lugosi) = 3.

In fact, there is a Web site at the University of Virginia (http://www.cs.virginia.edu/oracle/) that does nothing but maintain an in-memory graph database for just this single problem. It downloads current data from the Internet Movie Database (www.IMDb.com for the causual user and www.IMDbpro.com for someone who wants custom reports on over 7 million records for a monthly fee), which contain over 800,000 actors and actresses, over 375,000 movies, and over 70,000 aliases. It is a cute piece work for a single—and silly—purpose, but it is not a general tool.

The question is, can we do this kind of thing in standard SQL or a standard OLAP tool? Here is what I have come up with after more than 15 years of trying for an answer.

16.1 Adjacency List Model for General Graphs

First, I need to assume that you know something about Graph Theory. This is a branch of mathematics that deals with "nodes and edges" in 25 words or fewer. The nodes are abstract static places, and edges are relationships or flows between the nodes.

It is one of the most powerful mathematical tools we have, because it is so general. A road map's nodes are cities, and the edges are streets. A family tree's nodes are people, and the edges are blood relations. A circuit diagram's nodes are components, and the edges are the wires between them. They are so general; you have used them all your life but probably haven't thought of them in a formal sense.

The most common way to model a graph in SQL is an adjacency list model. It is also the best way I know to model a general graph. Some special kinds of graphs can be modeled differently (see my book *Trees & Hierarchies in SQL*, San Francisco, CA: Morgan-Kaufmann Publishers, 1999), but that is not the point of this chapter.

This is a typical adjacency list model of a general graph with one kind of edge that is understood from context. Structure goes in one table, and the nodes go in a separate table, because they are separate kinds of things (i.e., entities and relationships).

```
CREATE TABLE Actors
(actor_id CHAR(2) NOT NULL PRIMARY KEY);

CREATE TABLE MovieCasts
(begin_actor_id INTEGER NOT NULL
        REFERENCES Nodes (actor_id)
        ON UPDATE CASCADE
        ON DELETE CASCADE,
 end_actor_id INTEGER NOT NULL
         REFERENCES Nodes (actor_id)
        ON UPDATE CASCADE
        ON DELETE CASCADE,
 PRIMARY KEY (begin_actor_id, end_actor_id),
 CHECK (begin_actor_id <> end_actor_id));
```

A path through a graph is a traversal of consecutive nodes along a sequence of edges. Clearly, the node at the end of one edge in the sequence must also be the node at the beginning of the next edge in the sequence. The length of the path is the number of edges that are traversed along the path. In this particular problem, the nodes are actors and the edges are the "in a movie with" relationship.

I am looking for a path from "Kevin Bacon," who is 's' in my example data, to some other actor that has a length less than six. Actually, what I would really like is the shortest path within the set of paths between actors.

The advantage of SQL is that it is a declarative, set-oriented language. When I specify a rule for a path, I get all the paths in the set. That is a good thing—usually. However, it also means that we have to compute and reject or accept all possible candidate paths. This means a combinatorial explosion; the number of combinations you have to look at increases so fast that the time required to process them is beyond the computing capacity in the universe.

I made one decision that will be important later; I added self-traversal edges (i.e., an actor is always in a movie with himself) with zero length. I am going to use letters instead of actor names. We are looking at a mere five actors called {'s,' 'u,' 'v,' 'x,' 'y'}.

```
INSERT INTO Movies—15 edges
VALUES ('s,' 's'); ('s,' 'u'), ('s,' 'x'),
 ('u,' 'u'), ('u,' 'v'), ('u,' 'x'), ('v,' 'v'), ('v,' 'y'),
('x,' 'u'),
 ('x,' 'v'), ('x,' 'x'), ('x,' 'y'), ('y,' 's'), ('y,' 'v'),
('y,' 'y')
```

I am not happy about this approach, because I have to decide the maximum number of edges in the path before I start looking for an answer. But this will work, and I know that a path will have no more than the total number of nodes in the graph. Let's create a query of the paths:

```
CREATE TABLE Movies
(in_node CHAR(1) NOT NULL,
 out_node CHAR(1) NOT NULL)

INSERT INTO Movies
VALUES ('s,' 's'),, ('s,' 'u'), ('s,' 'x'),
                ('u,' 'u'), ('u,' 'v'), ('u,' 'x'), ('v,' 'v'),
                ('v,' 'y'), ('x,' 'u'), ('x,' 'v'), ('x,' 'x'),
                ('x,' 'y'), ('y,' 's'), ('y,' 'v';, ('y,' 'y');
```

```
CREATE TABLE Paths
(step1 CHAR(2) NOT NULL,
 step2 CHAR(2) NOT NULL,
 step3 CHAR(2) NOT NULL,
 step4 CHAR(2) NOT NULL,
 step5 CHAR(2) NOT NULL,
 path_length INTEGER NOT NULL,
PRIMARY KEY (step1, step2, step3, step4, step5));
```

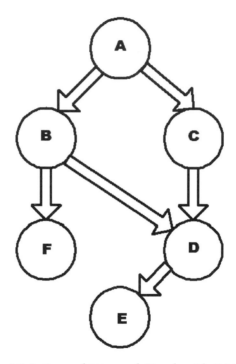

Figure 16.1 General Directed Graph with 6 Nodes

Figure 16.1 is a diagram of the six-node graph modeled in the table. Let's go to the query and load the table with all the possible paths of length five or less:

```
DELETE FROM Paths;
INSERT INTO Paths
SELECT DISTINCT M1.out_node AS s1, -- it is 's' in this example
       M2.out_node AS s2,
       M3.out_node AS s3,
       M4.out_node AS s4,
```

```
        M5.out_node AS s5,

        (CASE WHEN M1.out_node NOT IN (M2.out_node, M3.out_node,
M4.out_node, M5.out_node) THEN 1 ELSE 0 END
        + CASE WHEN M2.out_node NOT IN (M3.out_node, M4.out_node,
M5.out_node) THEN 1 ELSE 0 END
        + CASE WHEN M3.out_node NOT IN (M2.out_node, M4.out_node,
M5.out_node) THEN 1 ELSE 0 END
        + CASE WHEN M4.out_node NOT IN (M2.out_node, M3.out_node,
M5.out_node) THEN 1 ELSE 0 END
         + CASE WHEN M5.out_node NOT IN (
M2.out_node, M3.out_node, M4.out_node) THEN 1 ELSE 0 END)
        AS path_length
  FROM Movies AS M1, Movies AS M2, Movies AS M3, Movies AS M4,
Movies AS M5
 WHERE M1.in_node = M2.out_node
   AND M2.in_node = M3.out_node
   AND M3.in_node = M4.out_node
   AND M4.in_node = M5.out_node
   AND 0 < (CASE WHEN M1.out_node NOT IN (M2.out_node,
M3.out_node, M4.out_node, M5.out_node) THEN 1 ELSE 0 END
           + CASE WHEN M2.out_node NOT IN (M1.out_node,
M3.out_node, M4.out_node, M5.out_node) THEN 1 ELSE 0 END
           + CASE WHEN M3.out_node NOT IN (M1.out_node,
M2.out_node, M4.out_node, M5.out_node) THEN 1 ELSE 0 END
           + CASE WHEN M4.out_node NOT IN (M1.out_node,
M2.out_node, M3.out_node, M5.out_node) THEN 1 ELSE 0 END
           + CASE WHEN M5.out_node NOT IN (M1.out_node,
M2.out_node, M3.out_node, M4.out_node) THEN 1 ELSE 0 END);
SELECT * FROM Paths ORDER BY step1, step5, path_length;
```

"Step1" is where I begin the path. The other columns are the second step, third step, fourth step, and so forth. The last step column is the end of the journey. The SELECT DISTINCT is a safety attempt to catch cycles in the graph, and the "greater than zero" is to clean out the zero length "start to start" paths. This is a complex query, even by my standards.

The path length calculation is a bit harder. This sum of CASE expressions looks at each node in the path. If it is unique within the row, it is assigned a value of one; if it is not unique within the row, it is assigned a value of zero.

You will have 306 rows in the path table. But how many of these rows are actually the same path? SQL has to have a fixed number of columns in a table, but paths can be of different lengths. That is to say that $(s, y, y, y, y) = (s, s, y, y, y) = (s, s, s, y, y) = (s, s, s, s, y)$. A path is not supposed to have cycles in it, so you need to filter the answers. The only places for this are in the WHERE clause or outside of SQL in a procedural language.

Frankly, I found it was easier to do the filtering in a procedural language instead of SQL. Load each row into a linked list structure and use recursive code to find cycles. If you do it in SQL, you need a predicate for all possible cycles of size 1, 2, and so forth up to the number of nodes in the graph.

Magically assume that cycle removal is not a problem, but we are still dead. Extending this pattern for a graph in the real world, like streets in any major city, simply will not work. The number of rows from such queries increases drastically as the number of edges and nodes increases in the graph. The only way to handle this is to create a program to generate the n-column table declaration and the n-way self-join query. Or we can set a maximum depth and do a series of UNIONed queries, one per level.

16.2 Covering Paths Model for General Graphs

What if we attempt to store all the paths in a directed graph in a single table in an RDBMS? The table for this would look like this:

```
CREATE TABLE Path
(path_nbr INTEGER NOT NULL,
 step_nbr INTEGER NOT NULL
   CHECK (path_nbr >= 0),
 node_id CHAR(1) NOT NULL,
  PRIMARY KEY (path_nbr, step_nbr));
```

Each path is assigned an id number, and the steps are numbered from zero (the start of the path) to (k), the final step. Using the simple six-node graph, the one-edge paths are:

```
1 0 A
1 1 B
2 0 B
2 1 F
3 0 C
3 1 D
4 0 B
4 1 D
```

5 0 D
5 1 E

Now we can add the two-edge paths:

6 0 A
6 1 B
6 2 F
7 0 A
7 1 B
7 2 D
8 0 A
8 1 C
8 2 D
9 0 B
9 1 D
9 2 E

And, finally, the three-edge paths:

10 0 A
10 1 B
10 2 D
10 3 E
11 0 A
11 1 B
11 2 D
11 3 E

These rows can be generated from the single-edge paths using a CTE or with a loop in a procedural language, such as SQL/PSM. Obviously, there are fewer longer paths, but as the number of edges increases, so does the number of paths. By the time you get to a realistic-sized graph, the number of rows is huge. However, it is easy to find a path between two nodes:

```
SELECT :DISTINCT start_node, :end_node,
            (P2.step_nbr- P1.step_nbr) AS distance
  FROM Paths AS P1, Paths AS P2
 WHERE P1.path_nbr = P2.path_nbr
   AND P1.step_nbr <= P2.step_nbr
```

```
     AND P1.node_id = :start_node
     AND P2.node_id = :end_node;
```

Notice the use of SELECT DISTINCT, because most paths will be subpaths of one or more longer paths. Without it, the search for all paths from A to D in this simple graph would return:

```
7  0  A
7  1  B
7  2  D
8  0  A
8  1  C
8  2  D
10 0  A
10 1  B
10 2  D
11 0  A
11 1  B
11 2  D
```

However, there are only two distinct paths, namely (A, B, D) and (A, C, D). In a realistic graph with lots of connections, there is a good chance that a large percentage of the table will be returned.

Can we do anything to avoid the size problems? Yes and no.

In this graph, most of the paths are redundant and can be removed. Look for a set of subpaths that cover all of the paths in the original graph.

This is easy enough to do by hand for this simple graph:

```
1  0  A
1  1  B
1  2  F

2  0  A
2  1  B
2  2  D
2  3  E

3  0  A
3  1  C
3  2  D
3  3  E
```

The first observations are that if we have a cycle of size (k) in the graph, we would split it into two paths of (k–1) nodes that overlap. If the graph has cycles that overlap or form a lattice, the number of possible paths increases; notice the way that this graph has two paths between node A and D that split and reconverge.

I have no idea whether or not there is already a name in the literature for such a set of paths, so I will call it a "covering path set" and hope that it sticks. Furthermore, I have no idea how to construct it other than brute force—and no idea how to test that the set has the minimal number of paths or how to find all possible such sets other than brute force.

Apparently, I am not the only one. The problem of finding the longest path in a general graph is known to be *NP-Complete*, and finding the longest path is the first step of finding a minimal covering path set. For those of you without a computer science degree, NP-Complete problems are those that require drastically more resources (storage space and/or time) as the number of elements in the problem increases. There is usually an exhaustive search or combinatory explosion in these problems.

While search queries are easier in this model, dropping, changing, or adding a single edge can alter the entire structure, forcing us to rebuild the entire table. The combinatory explosion problem shows up again, so loading and validating the table takes too long for even a medium number of nodes.

16.3 Conclusion and Solution

My first conclusion is that it is possible to model a general graph in SQL, and my second conclusion is that it is not practical. You need a different kind of tool to find associations. The nature of a relational database is the assumption that the relationships are known in advance, so that a schema can be built and loaded with known facts. This is a good assumption in a production environment. Actually, it is a *necessary* assumption. You want to produce known and well-defined reports in an OLTP environment. Surprises are bad things and ad hoc reporting is handled with OLAP and reporting tools. But even OLAP deals with known relationships.

Now, consider another kind of data. You are a cop on a *CSI* show. All you have is a collection of odd facts that do not fall into nice neat relational tables. These facts tie various data elements together in various ways. You now have 60 minutes to find a network of associations to connect the bad guys to the crime in some as of yet unknown manner.

Ideally I would do a join between a table of "bad guys" and a table of "suspicious activities" on a known relationship. I have to know that such a join is possible before I can write the code. I have to insert my data into those tables as I collect it. I cannot whip up another relationship on the fly.

Let's consider an actual example. The police collect surveillance data in the form of notes and police reports. There is no fixed structure in which to fit this data. For example, U-Haul reports that a truck has not been returned, and the company files a police report. That same week, a farm supply company reports that someone purchased a large amount of ammonium nitrate fertilizer. If the same person did both actions, and used his or her own name (or a known alias) in both cases, then you could join them into a relationship based on the "bad guys" table. This would be fairly easy; you would have this kind of query in a VIEW for simple weekly reports. This is basically a shortest path problem, and it means that we are trying to find the dumbest terrorist in the United States.

In the real world, conspirator A rents the truck, and conspirator B buys the fertilizer. Or one guy rents a truck and cannot return it on time, while another totally unrelated person buys fertilizer. Who knows? To find out whether we have a coincidence or a conspiracy, we need a relationship between the people involved. That relationship can be weak (both people live in New York state) or strong (they were cellmates in prison).

The only tool I know that works for investigation and intelligence problems is Cogito (www.cogitoinc.com). The data is input as pairs of entities connected by a named relationship to build a general graph.

Look at the graph that was generated from the sample data of a missing rental truck and a fertilizer purchase (Figure 16.2). The result is a network that joins the truck to the fertilizer via two ex-cons, shared jail time, and a visit to a dam. Hey, that is a red flag for anyone! This kind of graph network is called a causal diagram in statistics and fuzzy logic. You will also see the same approach as a "fishbone diagram" when you are looking for patterns in data. Before now, this method has been a "scratch paper" technique. This is fine when you are working on one very dramatic case in a 60-minute police show and have a script writer.

In the real world, a major police department has a few hundred cases a week. The super-genius Sherlock Holmes characters are few and far between. But even if we could find such geniuses, we simply do not have

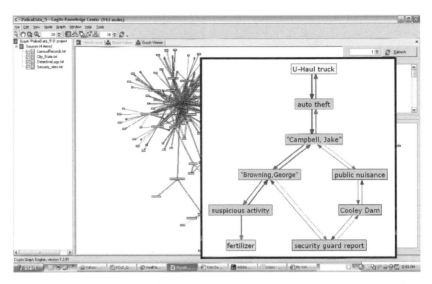

Figure 16.2 Cogito Relationship Query Result Windowed over the Entire Graph.

enough whiteboards to do this kind of analysis one case at a time in the real world. Intelligence must be computerized if it is going to work in the twenty-first century.

Most crimes are committed by repeat offenders. Repeat offenders tend to follow patterns—some of which are pretty horrible, if you look at serial killers. What a police department wants to do is describe a case and then look through all the open cases to see if there are three or more cases that have the same pattern.

Compare this to the evolution of mathematics. Arithmetic was like file systems—they summarize known values. Algebra was like RDBMS systems—they find values from known relationships. Cogito is like calculus—it finds relationships from atomic facts.

One major advantage is that data goes directly into the graph, while SQL requires that each new fact has to be checked against the existing data. I did a benchmark against a "Kevin Bacon" database. One test was to find the degrees with Kevin Bacon as "the center of the universe," and then a second test was to find a relationship between any two actors. We used 2,674,732 rows of data. Ignoring the time to set up the data, the query times for the simple Bacon numbers were:

Bacon Number	SQL	Cogito
1	00:00:24	0.172 Ms
2	00:02:06	00:00:13
3	00:12:52	00:00:01
4	00:14:03	00:00:13
5	00:14:55	00:00:16
6	00:14:47	00:00:43

The figures became much worse for SQL as we generalized the search (change the focus actor, use only actress links, use one common movie, and add directors). For example, changing the focus actor could be up to 9,000 times slower, and most were several hours versus times of less than one minute.

16.4 Further Reading

T. W. Anderson and J.D. Finn, *The New Statistical Analysis of Data*, New York: Springer, 1996.

F. Buckley and F. Harary, *Distance in Graphs*, Redwood City, CA: Addison-Wesley, 1990.

J. Celko, *Trees & Hierarchies in SQL*, San Francisco, CA: Morgan-Kaufmann Publishers, 1999.

R. M. Karp, "Reducibility Among Combinatorial Problems." In *Complexity of Computer Computations*, Proc. Sympos. IBM Thomas J. Watson Res. Center, Yorktown Heights, N.Y., R. E. Miller and J. W. Thatcher (eds.). New York: Plenum, 1972, pp. 85–103.

B. Kosko, *Fuzzy Thinking*, New York: Hyperion Press, 1993.

L. A. Levin, "Universal Searching Problems," *Prob. Info. Transm.*, Vol. 9, 1973, pp. 265–266.

C. H. Papadimitriou and K. Steiglitz, *Combinatorial Optimization: Algorithms and Complexity*, New York: Dover, 1998.

Other examples of specialized tools include DB2 Relationship Resolution and Inxight StarTree (www.inxight.com).

CHAPTER
17

Database Architectures

VLDB, WHICH STANDS for very large databases, is a specialized area in computer science. For a long time, VLDB stayed in academia and the military because nobody else had huge amounts of data. Then storage and processors got faster and cheaper, and it became easier to build custom hardware.

In the 1980s, there was a period of developing specialized database machines. The best-known companies were ShareBase (see Britton-Lee) and Teradata. Their products focused on decision support, rather than transaction processing. Teradata reached the market in 1984 with a database machine that could connect to IBM mainframes. Teradata acquired ShareBase in 1985. Other specialized machines included Red Brick, SAND Technology's SAND/DNA engines (see Nucleus Data), Tandem, Sequent, and White Cross.

Database machines could fill a niche, but they were too expensive for wide commercial use. However, they did lead to improvements in the general-purpose machines that could mimic some of the features of hardware.

I do not want to discuss particular machines, except as examples. This chapter is an overview of architectural principles as they apply to databases, and large databases in particular.

17.1 Parallelism

We can get a huge boost in power if our database can break a statement into disjoint sets, hand each part to its own processor, and then UNION the results back together. The important condition is that the problem can be made into disjoint sets. This is one of the advantages of a set-oriented language. However, if the task has steps that have to be done in a particular order, parallelism can actually cost execution time.

Tandem Computers, later bought out by Compaq in 1997, manufactured a line of fault-tolerant computers. Gus Baird used to explain the concept to his classes at Georgia Tech by telling them that a dog is fault tolerant and a horse is not—break a dog's leg, and it limps; break a horse's leg, and you have to shoot it. Their Non-Stop system had redundant processors and access paths, so that if one processor or access path failed, the hardware would pick up the same program and keep running. In fact, it required a special command (ambush) to kill both processors at the same. They added a SQL product and moved to off-the-shelf hardware.

White Cross is a British company that built parallel database servers from available hardware. Their WX9010 data exploration system ran 48 processors in parallel with SQL as the "native language" for the interface (much like Algol on the Burroughs 5000 computers). The throughput was about 20 million rows of data each second for a project at ScottishPower, a power company in the United Kingdom.

Teradata makes heavy use of parallelism, I want to use their product as an example of hashing.

17.1.1 Parallelism Failures

Parallelism can fail to improve performance when tasks have to be done in a particular order. Assume I have a list of nine tasks, T1 to T9, and their execution times. They are submitted in numeric order to three processors.

```
T1 = 3
T2 = 2
T3 = 2
T4 = 2
T5 = 4
T6 = 4
T7 = 4
T8 = 4
T9 = 9
```

Assume the dependency graph looks like Figure 17.1.

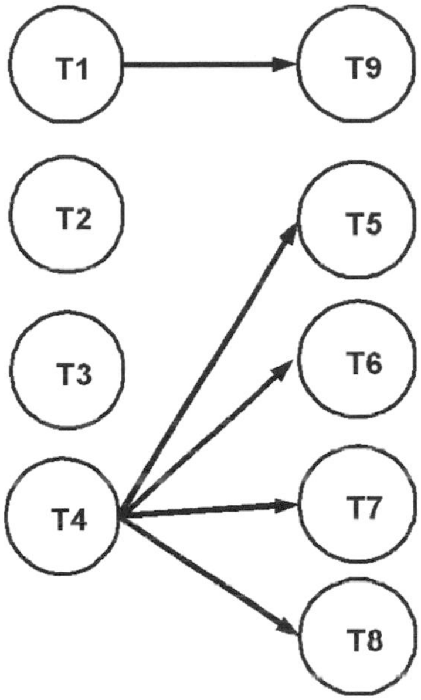

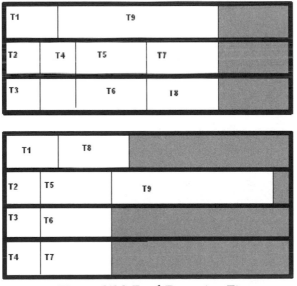

Figure 17.1 Tasks Dependence Graph.

When we put the task into three-processor and four-processor systems, the four-processor system takes longer to run the batch of tasks (see Figure 17.2).

Figure 17.2 Total Execution Times.

Other arrangements of dependencies and task lengths can produce counter-intuitive results, such as shortening all the tasks, requiring more overall time.

17.2 Hashing

Hashing takes a key and performs a function on it that produces an address in a lookup table. This table (which is not a table in the relational sense) has the physical location of the desired data, and we can access it directly. Compare this to how a tree-structured index works.

In a tree-structured index, we start at the root of the tree and follow paths to a leaf node, which has the physical location of the desired data. If we use a binary tree of (n) rows, then our expected search time is $\log_2(n)$ probes. We get flatter, faster search trees with n-ary trees, but all indexing suffers the same problem. As the number of nodes increases, the depth of the index tree increases, and so does the search time.

Writing hashing functions is not easy. If two or more values have the same hash value ("hash clash" or "collision"), then they are put into the same "bucket" in the hash table, or they are run through a second hashing function.

If the index is on a unique column, the ideal situation is what is called a minimal perfect hashing function—each value hashes to a unique physical storage address, and there are no empty spaces in the hash table. There are several research projects on this topic for use in databases.

The next-best situation for a unique column is what is called a perfect hashing function—every value hashes to one physical storage address without collisions, but there are some empty spaces in the physical hash table storage.

A hashing function for a nonunique column should ideally hash to a bucket small enough to fit into main storage or small enough for a single processor in a multiprocessor system. In the Teradata SQL engine, which is based on hashing, any row can be found in at most two probes, and 90% or more of the accesses require only one probe.

An advantage of hashing is that you can immediately reject buckets that do not have what you are looking for. The buckets that do have items of interest can be sent to their own processor and returned as soon as they are completed.

The problem is in the hashing algorithm. When you start to get too many clashes, it is time to rehash the table. The good news is that this can be done in one pass for statistics and one to change the hash codes.

Reindexing can take longer. However, for data warehouses, the data is static, so once the hash is done it will not need to be changed.

Teradata has several other unique performance-enhancing features that I will not cover here.

17.3 Bit Vector Indexes

The most popular product that uses bit vectors is Microsoft's FoxPro, an XBase product. The idea is to build a vector of bits in which each position represents the occurrence of a value in a column of a particular row in a table. Predicates are handled by doing Boolean bit operations on the arrays.

The advantages are that the index is small and that bit operations are fast and can do long strings of bits in the hardware. The proprietary SAND technology engine goes one step further. It uses a compressed format that can be manipulated, uncompressed, and displayed. The model is a 3D bit space made up of domains, rows, and columns. Tables are assembled column by column, which is confusing to programmers who are used to contiguous row storage in traditional file systems. The result is that the database is smaller than the original data and can be compressed even further if fast access is not required.

17.4 Streaming Databases

Streaming databases are fairly new. Kx Systems and StreamBase are the two commercial products at this time. The idea is to capture the data as it flows thru the system by using a lot of main storage to take snapshots in real time. You need a stream of data, such as the stock market, commodities, and other financial feeds, which has to be queried as it occurs. The data is passed through main storage in a window where it can be queried and then persisted to permanent storage.

This is a modification of in-memory databases, which try to get all the data into the main storage to make searching faster by not requiring conventional indexes or access methods.

Oracle bought TimesTen on June 20, 2005. This is an in-memory database product. ANTs is another in-memory database.

17.5 Further Reading

Best Practices (DM REVIEW, January 1998, ISSN 1521-2912)

StreamBase Systems, Inc.
181 Spring Street
Lexington, Massachusetts 02421
http://www.streambase.com/

Kx Systems, Inc.
555 Bryant Street #375
Palo Alto, CA 94301-1704
http://www.kx.com/

SAND Technology Inc.
215 Redfern, Westmount #410
Westmount, Quebec H3Z 3L5
http://www.sand.com/

NCR World Headquarters
Teradata Division
1700 S. Patterson Blvd.
Dayton, OH 45479
http://www.teradata.com/

CHAPTER 18

MDX from a SQL Viewpoint

MULTIDIMENSIONAL EXPRESSIONS (MDX) is a programming language that is part of the Microsoft OLAP SQL Server offering. Like many of Microsoft's products, it is a de facto industry standard due to Microsoft's marketing and a lower price point than its traditional competition.

This is a very quick overview of the MDX language from the viewpoint of a SQL programmer. I have tried to provide some BNF (Backus Normal Form) syntax and simple examples from the sample database, but I tried to rewrite some of the data element names to conform to SQL conventions, rather than OO conventions.

MDX uses square brackets for data element names that would otherwise be illegal. They serve the same purpose as double quotes in standard SQL but match the convention in other proprietary Microsoft languages. They also make it much more difficult to give a BNF definition of the language, so I have avoided using them in my examples.

18.1 MDX SELECT Statement

The keywords for the MDX "SELECT... FROM... WHERE..." statement were taken from the SQL SELECT statement, but they are nothing alike.

A cube or hypercube is viewed as being made up of the following five axes, based on terms used in a spreadsheet model. They have an ordering for display purposes.

```
SELECT <axis spec> ON COLUMNS,
       [<axis spec> ON ROWS,
        [<axis spec> ON PAGES,
         [<axis spec> ON CHAPTERS,
          [<axis spec> ON SECTIONS]]]]
  FROM <cube name>
 WHERE <slicer spec>
```

The SELECT clause gives us the values that will be displayed. However, the values can be a dimensional hierarchy over the axis. For example, I can have columns that show first race, then sex within each race, and then rows that show annual income.

The MDX FROM clause holds the name of the source cube, much like table expression in SQL's FROM clause.

The WHERE clause holds a slicer specification. In SQL, the WHERE clause would be a search condition. A slicer does not change the axis members, but the values that go into them. A filter, on the other hand, removes the members from the output.

The SELECT statements are similar, but not the same. A SQL query produces a table, while MDX produces a cube as a result.

A chain of names connected by dots gives a path through a dimensional hierarchy. Thus, "Time.YR1997" is the subset of the time dimension for the year 1997. I could add quarters within the year, months within a quarter, then days within a month. The language has keywords for traversing the dimensional hierarchies.

Stores.store_state.CA returns all the stores in California.

Stores.MEMBERS returns a set of elements at one level in the Stores dimension hierarchy.

Stores.CHILDREN returns a set of all the immediate subordinates in the Stores dimension.

DESCENDANTS (<member>, <level>, [,<flags>]) returns a set of all the subordinates in the Stores dimension. This is the "drill-down, drill-up" operator, and it has several options that I will not discuss. These determine whether you get (n) levels of subordinates, superiors, or both.

IMS and older nonrelational programmers will recognize this model of data from their navigational database languages.

Curly braces "{}" represent a set of members of a dimension or group of dimensions. This is taken from set theory notation.

MDX also has a WITH clause that looks like the CTE in SQL. The syntax is not quite the same. In SQL, the CTE is a "local, temporary view," which may or may not be materialized within the scope of the query. In MDX, it is enclosed in single quote marks, like an inline macro string. The syntax is:

```
WITH <parent>.<name> AS '<expression>'
    [, FORMAT_STRING '<format exp>'][SOLVE_ORDER = <positive
integer>]
 [, ...]
```

This will compute the expression, make it part of the <parent>, give it the name <name>, and let us use it. Think of a computed column in a CTE that is given a name. There is an option to use a CREATE statement and make this computed column available for all the MDX expressions in the session—the MDX version of a VIEW. Here is a short example:

```
WITH MEMBERS profit_percentage
AS 'measures.store_sales - measures.store_costs)
    / measures.store_costs', FORMAT_STRING '#.00%'
```

This will add a column for the percentage of profitability to a cube that has performance measurements in a dimension. The FORMAT_STRING option is a leftover from the spreadsheet heritage, in which cell-level formatting and display part of the language.

There is also a SOLVE_ORDER option, which will make are SQL programmer sick. It tells the engine to process the computations in a fixed order rather than "in parallel" or to let an optimizer decide.

Spreadsheet programmers are not alarmed. Order of execution was a big issue in the early days of spreadsheets. Do you compute the cells all at once as with SQL? What if I get an endless loop of references? Should I do it from left to right, then top to bottom—or top to bottom, then left to right? How many times should I recompute the spreadsheet?

There is also related syntax to generate a new set based on structural features in the data. This might be easier to explain with an example:

```
WITH SET Q1
AS 'GENERATE time_dim.sale_year,
        {time_dim.CURRENTMEMBER.FIRSTCHILD})'
```

Creating a member is not enough to display it. You must use an additional ADDCALCULATEDMEMBERS (add calculated members) function in the SELECT list. Here is an example:

```
SELECT ADDCALCULATEDMEMBERS (Mesures.MEMBERs)
        ON COLUMN,
{store.store_state.CA,
 DESCENDANTS (store.store_state.CA, store_city)}
        ON ROWS
    FROM Sales
```

18.2 Hierarchical Navigation

Older programmers who have worked with IMS, IDMS, and other navigational databases will see parallels in the following set of operators. The names explain themselves to some extent. IDMS (Integrated Database Management System) is a (network) CODASYL database management system first developed at B.F. Goodrich and later marketed by Cullinane Database Systems (renamed Cullinet in 1983). Since 1989 the product has been owned by Computer Associates, who renamed it Advantage CA-IDMS.

CURRENTMEMBER is the current member, and it is the reference point for the other navigational operators. For example, this expression will compute which percentage of sales a given product has within its category:

```
WITH MEMBER Measues.percent_in_category
AS '(Products.CURRENTMEMBER, Measures.unit_sales)
   /(Products.CURRENTMEMBER.PARENT, Measures.unit_sales)'
```

PARENT references the immediate superior of the CURRENTMEMBER of the hierarchy.

You can repeat PARENT.PARENT. . . . .PARENT to "climb up the tree," but a better and more general way is the ANCESTOR() function, which is a shorthand for this kind of operation. Notice how the language jumps from a postfixed notation to a function call.

You can find subordinates of the current member with the CHILDREN, FIRSTCHILD, and LASTCHILD operators. There is an assumption that the children are ordered under their parent.

Likewise, the siblings at the same level are referenced by PREVMEMBER, NEXTMEMBER, LAG(n), and LEAD(n) operators. PREVMEMBER is the same as LEAD(–1), and NEXTMEMBER is the same as LEAD(1). LAG(n)is the same as LEAD(–n). The usual purpose of these operators is a comparison over time, where you want to compare the same measurements over a series of years or other reporting periods. However, MDX has a collection of temporal functions that form ranges, which we will discuss later.

18.3 Set Operations

SQL-92 added UNION [ALL], INTERSECT [ALL], and EXCEPT [ALL] as infixed set operators that manipulate tables as sets. MDX has only the EXCEPT operation and changed the syntax to functional notation: EXCEPT(<named set1>, <named set2> [,ALL]).

In fairness, I am not quite sure what a UNION or INTERSECTION of a cube would mean. MDX also includes a CROSSJOIN() function that will produce all possible pairs of values.

18.4 GENERATE Function

The GENERATE function builds a new set from the members of another set—for example:

```
{GENERATE ({store.CA, store.WA},
      DESCENDANTS(store.CURRENTMEMBER, store_name))}
```

The first set gets us California and Washington State stores. Then the second parameter fills those states and produces the names of the stores by using the elements of the first set as the CURRENTMEMBER.

18.5 Time Series Functions

MDX has a set of functions that block off ranges of time for reporting. The first subgroup of these functions is the "Period To Date," which includes the following:

- YTD = year to date

- MTD = month to date

- QTD = quarter to date

- WTD = week to date

The other subgroup is the "period family," which includes the following:

- PARALLELPERIOD allows us to compare corresponding members in two periods. For example, how do third-quarter sales this year compare to third-quarter sales last year?

- OPENINGPERIOD and CLOSINGPERIOD give us the extreme limits of a temporal unit, like the first and last months in a quarter.

- PERIODTODATE explains itself.

18.6 Filtering

Slicing a cube keeps all the members in an axis, even if they do not hold data. For example, I might have no sales for next month, but I have a slot for that data in my cube.

Filtering removes members from an axis. You generally would do this to get rid of those empty members. The special function for this cleanup is:

```
NON EMPTY <set>
```

Again, notice the spreadsheet model of data; we talk about empty cells rather than NULLs, and this syntax breaks the pattern of single word function names.

The more general form of filter is:

```
FILTER (<set>, <search condition>)
```

The search condition is pretty much what you would expect in any programming language. It has the usual infixed comparison operators, simple math, and so forth.

18.7 ORDER ()

Unlike SQL, the MDX sets can be ordered. Again, we see a SQL keyword being converted into a function instead of a clause. The syntax is:

```
ORDER (<set>, <expression> [,ASC | DESC | BASC | BDESC]
```

The ASC and DESC options are for ascending and descending orderings at each level of the hierarchy. The <expression> is the sort key. This is how most people want to see a report.

The BASC and BDESC options are for breaking the hierarchical ordering so the sort is done with without regard to levels within the set.

18.8 TOP Functions

Another family of functions picks out the greatest (n) values from a set. SQL Server has a proprietary "SELECT TOP n" extension, and other SQL products have clauses to limit the number of rows returned.

HEAD(<set>, <n>) assumes an ordering in a set and returns the first (n) members. There is also a TAIL() function, which returns the members that are not in the head. Usually, there will be an ORDER() on the set to assure that the HEAD() makes sense. As an aside, these terms are used in list processing languages and not with databases at all.

TOPCOUNT() also returns the top (n) with slightly different syntax. For example, the set of five stores with the highest volume can be done with this:

```
WITH SET BestStores
AS 'TOPCOUNT(Stores.store_city.MEMBERS, 5, sales_volume)'
```

The family also includes TOPPERCENT() and TOPSUM(), along with a matching group of BOTTOM functions.

18.9 Numeric Functions

A family of numeric functions is available in SQL, but is once more given an MDX twist. The functions are all of the form (<set>, <numeric expression>), where the operation is done on a subset of values in the set and the <numeric expression> controls the size of that subset.

- SUM() and AVG() are summation and the average of the set respectively.

- MEDIAN() is the median.

- MAX() and MIN() are the minimum and maximum values in the set.

- STDDEV and VAR() are the standard deviation and the variance.

- The COUNT(<set>, <numeric expression> [, EXCLUDEEMPTY]) function has an option to ignore the empty cells in the count, much the way as COUNT(*) in SQL counts NULLs and COUNT(<expression>) ignores them.

- There is also an IIF() function, which acts like a small version of the SQL CASE expression but with functional syntax. The COALESCEEMPTY() function is a version of the SQL COALESCE(), which works on empty cells.

- If this is not enough power for us, we can also link in Visual BASIC functions to MDX.

18.10 Conclusions

MDX syntax is a nightmare mix of a Microsoft OO language, IMS-style hierarchical navigation, set theory notations, bracketing of various symbols, and standard SQL keywords used in new ways. It is based on cube manipulations (slicing, drilling) and a spreadsheet model. Terminology is borrowed from mixed sources, as is syntax.

The result is that if you do not memorize the syntax, you will not be able to easily guess at what to write. People do not write much MDX—they use the GUI tools to build reports.

Having said all of this, we are stuck with MDX until open source or an industry standard comes along with an easier language. Bits and pieces of OLAP are showing up in SQL, but it is not a full product yet.

Index

Joe Celko is a noted consultant and lecturer, and one of the most-read SQL authors in the world. He is well known for his 10 years of service on the ANSI SQL standards committee, his column in *Intelligent Enterprise* magazine (which won several Reader's Choice Awards), and the war stories he tells to provide real-world insights into SQL programming. His best-selling books include *Joe Celko's SQL for Smarties: Advanced SQL Programming, second edition; Joe Celko's SQL Puzzles and Answers;* and *Joe Celko's Trees and Hierarchies in SQL for Smarties.*